LOST
COUNCIL BLUFFS

S.M. SENDEN

THE History PRESS

Published by The History Press
Charleston, SC
www.historypress.net

Cover image: One of the electric trolley cars that transported citizens about the city.

First published 2016

Manufactured in the United States

ISBN 978.1.46713.747.8

Library of Congress Control Number: 2016945800

To all those people, past, present and future, who are woven into the fabric of Council Bluffs.

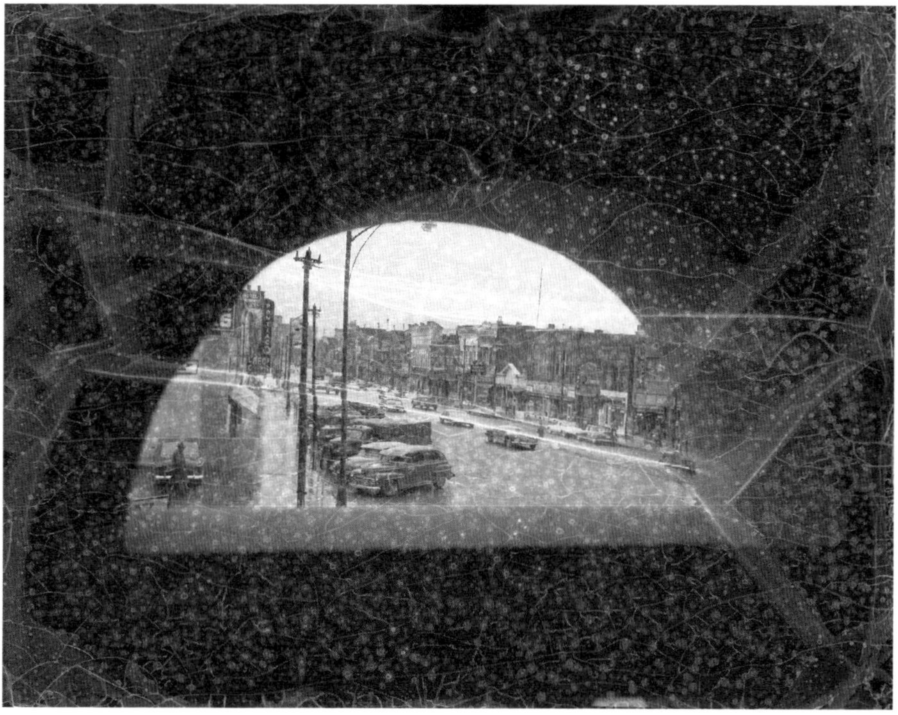

Broadway through a half-moon window in 1950, as through a glass darkly. Within twenty years, the downtown would change irrevocably in the name of urban renewal.

CONTENTS

Preface	7
PART I. FLEDGLING OUTPOST	9
PART II. A LITTLE MORMON SETTLEMENT	14
PART III. CHANGING HANDS	20
The Lore of the Ocean Wave	23
Indian Creek	31
PART IV. LAW AND ORDER	33
Postal Office and Federal Building	35
County Courthouse and Jail	40
City Hall and Jail	45
Police Department	47
Fire Department	53
PART V. HOTELS	63
Pacific House	73
The Neumayer	80
Ogden House	83

CONTENTS

Part VI. Entertainment 89
Dohany Opera House 91

Part VII. Businesses and Buildings 99
John G. Woodward & Co. 102
John Beno & Co. 104
Masonic Temple 108
J.F. Wilcox, Florist 109
Merriam Block 111
Banking Houses 115
Newspapers 118

Part VIII. Urban Renewal 122

Bibliography 127
About the Author 128

PREFACE

This book presents only a fraction of the historic buildings Council Bluffs has lost over the years as the city has changed, grown and reinvented itself anew with each generation. As with any village, town or city that is vibrant and growing, nothing remains the same. Change is inevitable. For Council Bluffs, the transformations happened in successive waves. The old buildings were razed to make way for the new. The log cabin homes and businesses that the first settlers built were soon replaced by larger, more modern frame buildings, and subsequently, brick buildings replaced most of those. Even the buildings considered cutting edge in their day have been replaced again and again by newer, more modern structures. Only when this process ends does a city come to the end of its life. Council Bluffs is far from the end of its days.

The history of Council Bluffs is reflected in the buildings constructed over the years. Records of successive generations overlay one another as the years pass. The history isn't a linear, neatly ordered document. It is a series of occurrences, interwoven by lives, events and structures that overlap, coincide and juxtapose. Sometimes it is difficult to decipher those records of the past—to reconstruct, to sort through faulty and fading memories, gossip and confusion that overlies the truth. Memories diminish, become confused and conflated. Much of this history may be familiar; we caress those well-told stories for generations. A tapestry woven of lives and events has been passed down to us, and we are part of it today. Soon, our lives will be woven into the fabric of the historical record that is Council Bluffs so that future generations will look back nostalgically as they forge a new present and future. As we look back at buildings that have been lost, perhaps we can rediscover and treasure those that remain and try to preserve them for future generations as living history of the growth of the city. Old and new can stand next to each other.

The names, locations and dates of people, places and buildings at times conflict; other times, they coincide with one another. Some people's names, once prominent in the growth of the city, may have been pushed aside and forgotten for deeds that were not considered positive in the past. However, those are the characters who give color and richness to the growth of any metropolis. In doing this research, I have found at least one man whose varied past has been omitted, yet without his actions, the fate of the city may have been very different.

Those of us who relate these histories spend many hours in painstaking research, reading and rereading old documents, publications, diaries, newspaper articles, et cetera. The past captures our imaginations. It gets under our skin; it haunts our dreams as we begin to open the doors of history in the dusty old records, photos and writings of those who went before us. As a historian, and as historians before me, my work is to attempt to unravel the tangled skein of the threads of the past and hopefully weave them into a tapestry, giving a picture that invites the reader to enter, remember and tell the stories again to the next generation. As an apologia, please forgive any errors and know that this book represents only a portion of the buildings lost throughout the history of Council Bluffs.

As with any book, there are many people who have helped make it a reality. No author works completely alone, especially on a book like this. Special thanks to Kathy Reiger, Mary Carpenter and Ben Johnson at the Council Bluffs Public Library. If you are unfamiliar with the vast and wonderful collection of photos, documents and memorabilia we have at the library, I would urge you to spend a few hours captivated by the past. But be careful, you may get lost in the pages that bring the past to life once again.

Thanks also to Sister and Elder Whittle of Utah and Sister Lang, who were great helps at the Mormon Tabernacle, presenting their early history and answering my many questions. And thanks to Calvin J. Petersen for allowing me to use some of his wonderful photos and steering me in the direction of his book about the history of fires in Council Bluffs. Thanks also to Officer Dave Burns for his kind loan of a *Selected History of the Council Bluffs Police Department.* Thanks to the Nonpareil photograph archives, also at the library. And of course, thanks to my editor, Edward Mack, always patient and helpful as we created this book.

Please note that photographs in this volume are primarily from the collection of the Council Bluffs Public Library unless marked as CBPD for the Council Bluffs Police Department or CBFD-Petersen for Cal Petersen's photos of fires and historic photographs of the fire department.

I

FLEDGING OUTPOST

Imagine a great number of cabins and tents, made of bark of trees, buffalo skins, coarse cloth, rushes and sods, all of a mournful and funeral aspect of all sizes and shapes, some supported by one pole, others having six, and with the covering stretched in all different styles imaginable, and all scattered here and there in the greatest confusion, and you will have an Indian village.
—E. Laville, The Life of Father De Smet, *1915*

The size of the nation doubled when President Thomas Jefferson bought lands from France. These new lands needed to be explored, mapped and documented. President Jefferson commissioned Captain Meriwether Lewis and William Clark to explore the lands of the Louisiana Purchase. On August 4, 1804, on their Corps of Discovery Expedition, they recorded a meeting with the Oto and Missouri at the foot of a high promontory on the banks of the Missouri River. The designation of this place was called the Council Bluff and was later adopted by traders, trappers and river navigators to describe the area on both sides of the Missouri River.

When Iowa Territory opened, the majority of settlements grew on the banks of the Mississippi River. People looked to the interior and western edge of Iowa Territory as a place no one would want to settle and deemed the land of little use. They had the Mississippi as their highway for trade and travel. In the western edge of the territory, the Omaha, Otoe and Miami Nations resided. This attitude was soon to change.

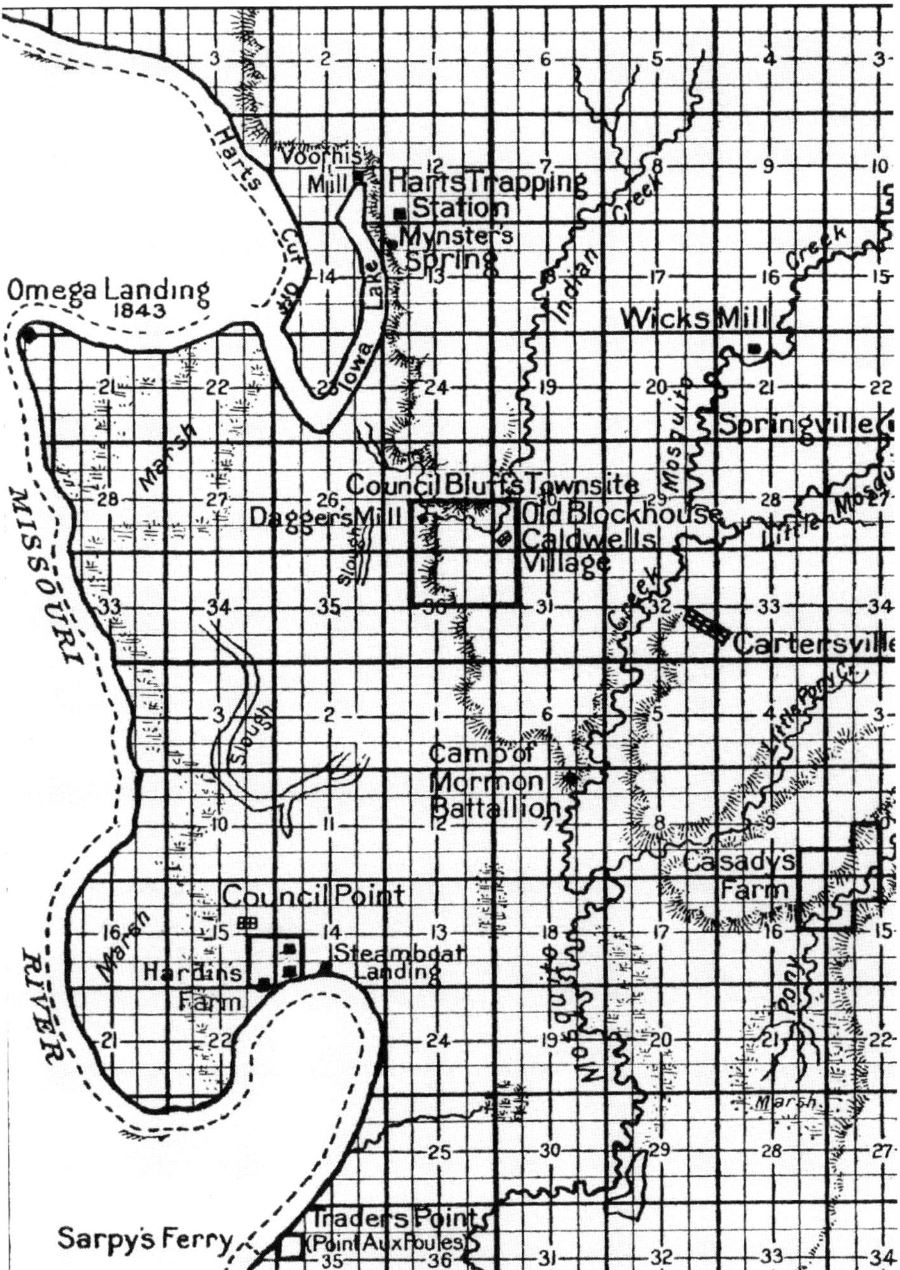

A map illustrating Hart's Cut-Off, Iowa Lake, blockhouse and Billy Caldwell's settlement. Traders Point, Council Point, the steamboat landing.

One of the first names given to the area was Hart's Bluff, named for a fur trapping station. The ever-changing banks of the muddy Missouri River created another channel that began to silt in, as noted on a surprisingly accurate map drawn by David H. Burr in 1840 that showed Hart's Cut-Off on the Missouri. The map named the channel Iowa Lake (it later silted in and became what we currently call the Big Lake). At the top of this lake, Hart's Trapping Station and the Voorhis mill were located. Mynster Springs, where Mr. Mynster and his wife, Maria, settled, was located below the lake. The map also shows the Council Bluffs town site, the Old Blockhouse and Caldwell's Village, which sat along Indian Creek. This was regarded as the only civilian village between Leavenworth and Fort Mandam, near current-day Bismark, South Dakota.

Charles Babbitt did extensive research on the name of Hart in old American Fur Company records (as it had the monopoly of trading in America) and found no record of a white man by that name. Old legend relates that Hart was an Iowa Indian chief who gave his name to the area, as described in notes by Dr. Edwin James, secretary on an 1819–20 expedition to the Rocky Mountains under the leadership of Stephen H. Long.

François Guittar, a teenage cook on the boat belonging to the American Fur Company, recalls one of his first trips up the river in 1824, when they came ashore at Trader's Point. There, Peter Sarpy established his trading post on the western bank of the Missouri River. Sarpy's trading post later became the town of Bellevue, Nebraska. By 1826, Guittar had set up his own trading post at Trader's Point and became a trusted trader, dealer and counselor to the Indians. Later, he settled in the young town that became Council Bluffs, opening a store that traded with Native Americans.

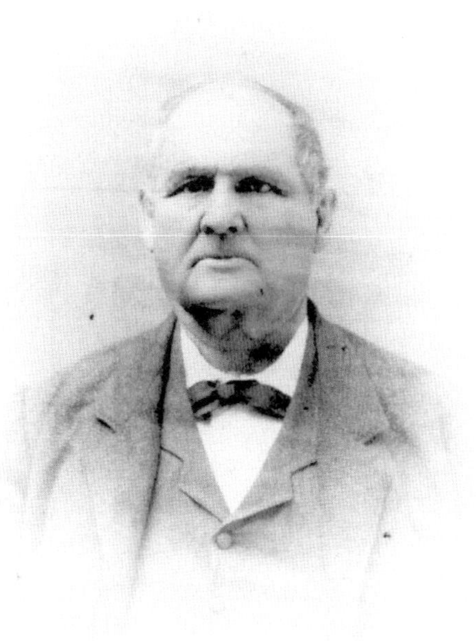

Early pioneer François Guittar worked on riverboats, ran a trading post and settled in Council Bluffs to run an Indian grocery store on Broadway.

In 1837, about 2,700 Pottawattamie, Ottawa and Chippewa were relocated to the area along the Missouri River from Chicago. Billy Caldwell, also known as Chief Sauganash, a peacemaker and respected man, led his people to the new area granted to them by treaty. He was the mixed-race son of Irish immigrant William Caldwell (also called Billy Caldwell) and a Mohawk mother. He won admiration in the War of 1812.

The Indians settled along the Missouri River in smaller groups. Billy Caldwell and about five hundred of his people settled on a valley floor nestled into the Loess Hills, a prominent geological feature in the area. Indian Creek meandered through the settlement. They built "wickiups" and some log cabins with the assistance of the army. They referred to their settlement as Caldwell's Camp. The U.S. Dragoons built a small fort nearby to keep the peace between the peaceful Pottawattamie and the aggressive Sioux Nation to the north. This company of Dragoons from Fort Leavenworth, under Captain D.B. Moore, arrived on July 27, 1837, and spent the next three months building a twenty-four-foot-square blockhouse on a commanding hill overlooking the settlement.

Steamboat traffic up and down the Missouri brought provisions. Too often, those provisions included alcohol. In late May 1838, nearly two thousand ceremonially dressed Native Americans came to Trader's Point to greet the steamboat *Howard*, expecting alcohol, as the whiskey trade was flourishing and preyed on Indians. Instead of alcohol, they were greeted by Catholic missionaries. Father Pierre-Jean De Smet, Father Felix Verrydt and a lay brother, Mr. Mazelli, arrived to minister to the Pottawattamie, convert them to Christianity and establish a mission church and school.

Chief Caldwell made the missionaries welcome and offered them some of the rough cabins the soldiers had constructed. In 1838–39, missionary Pierre-Jean De Smet claimed the blockhouse and founded St. Joseph's Mission to minister to the Pottawattamie. De Smet had permission to use the blockhouse and immediately placed a cross atop the roof, proclaiming it a church.

The St. Joseph's Mission School had thirty boys enrolled. He had little success converting the Pottawattamie to Christianity. De Smet claimed 118 baptisms, though it was said he did secret baptisms of the children to "save their souls" from damnation.

As part of his work, he tried to protect the people from the unscrupulous whiskey traders and the violence that broke out among them after drinking "the firewater." During his time there, he fought the whiskey trade, proclaiming it to be "a war of extermination" waged on the Pottawattamie. Thirty-gallon barrels of whiskey, brandy, rum or other alcohol would come up the river, available for sale to the Pottawattamie.

By 1841, the mission school had been abandoned, as De Smet was sent elsewhere to continue his work. He contributed to the cartography efforts of Joseph Nicollet as he mapped the upper Midwest. De Smet made the first European-recorded and detailed maps of the Council Bluffs area, showing the Missouri River Valley system from below the Platt to the Big Sioux River.

As white men settled more land, they displaced Native American populations who had been granted lands not deemed valuable at the time. Inter-tribal conflicts increased, fueled by the illegal whiskey trade, causing friction among nations, as well as with the white traders who, more and more, utilized the rivers and built trading posts. In 1842, the U.S. Army built Fort Croghan to keep order and try to control the liquor traffic along the Missouri River. This log fort was flooded out with the rising level of the Missouri, and the men moved to higher ground.

In 1844, the Stephens-Murphy party crossed the Missouri River at Council Bluffs hoping to blaze a new path to California across the Sierra Nevada. This would have unimagined repercussions for the future of the remote settlement nestled within the embrace of the bluffs.

In 1846, the Pottawattamie again were relocated to the Kansas Territory under a new treaty. They sold their lands back to the government and relocated along the Kansas River, abandoning the town site.

II

A LITTLE MORMON SETTLEMENT

A squalid looking collection of log cabins—many of them with dirt roofs—at the base of those lofty bluffs which bound the river valley on the east...one street contained the stores, saloons, and most of the residences.
—W.H. Taft recalls his first sighting of Kanesville, circa 1850s

The recently abandoned village did not remain empty for long. Following the violent hostilities in Navoo, Illinois, the Mormons arrived in the area that encompassed Billy Cladwell's settlement on Indian Creek. Beginning in June 1846, a large influx of Latter-day Saints arrived, many wintering in the area before they would make the long journey to the Great Salt Lake Brigham Young had chosen for their settlement, where hatred, fear and prejudice would not hamper their chosen practices and worship.

The Mormons named the area Miller's Hollow, after Henry W. Miller, who enlisted the help of others to build the tabernacle. The large log structure was erected in two and a half weeks. In this tabernacle, they carried on the important business of securing Brigham Young as their profit, succeeding Joseph Smith, who had been murdered in Navoo.

Apostle Orson Hyde led another group of settlers to the area, arriving on July 21, 1846. The Mormons fixed up existing log cabins, built other shelters and planted crops, as they expected more waves of Mormon migrants to arrive before heading west to the Great Salt Lake, then a part of Mexico. Many lived in their wagons or pitched tents, as there wasn't sufficient housing for the thousands of people who came to the area. Temporary

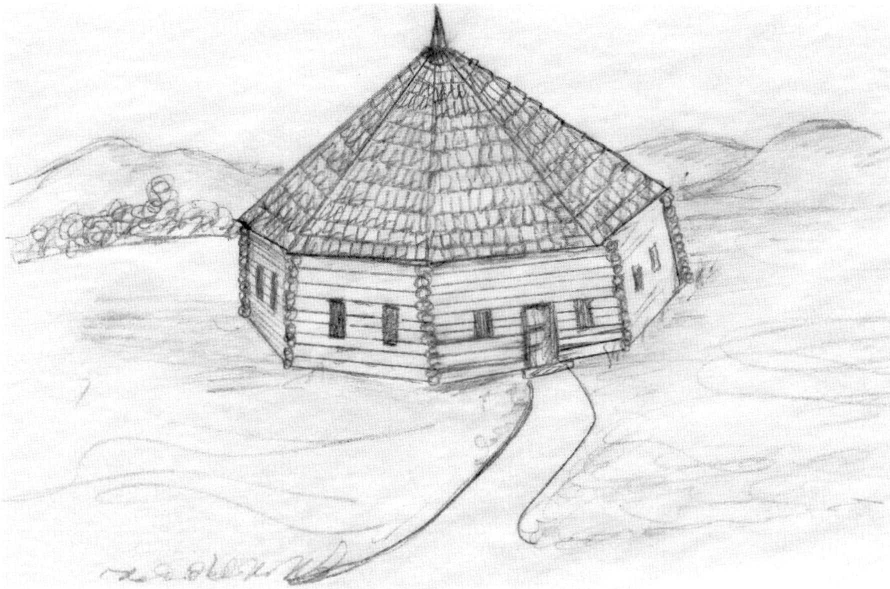

The Mormon tabernacle, built of logs in two and a half weeks by Elder Miller and two hundred men. The Mormons named their settlement Miller's Hollow in his honor.

winter quarters were also established across the river in what later became Florence, Nebraska.

The Mormons set up a municipal government on July 21, 1846, on a hill they called Council Point. Many built homes and established businesses that would supply the waves of migrants traveling to Utah. Orson Hyde built his log home at Washington and Harmony Streets.

On February 17, 1848, Brigham Young petitioned Congress for a post office under the name of Kane. Soon after the government awarded them the post office, on April 8, 1848, the Mormons changed the name of the town from Miller's Hollow to Kanesville. They named the town site for Thomas L. Kane. He had helped them negotiate in Washington, D.C., obtaining federal permission for the Mormons to use Indian lands along the Missouri River for winter encampments and build alongside Caldwell's Camp.

Kanesville became the main outfitting post for the Mormons traveling to Utah. In the spring of 1848, Brigham Young and four thousand other people left for the Salt Lake. Council Bluffs was the head of the Mormon trail. In many advertisements between 1849 and 1852, the area was referred to as Kanesville and also as Council Bluffs.

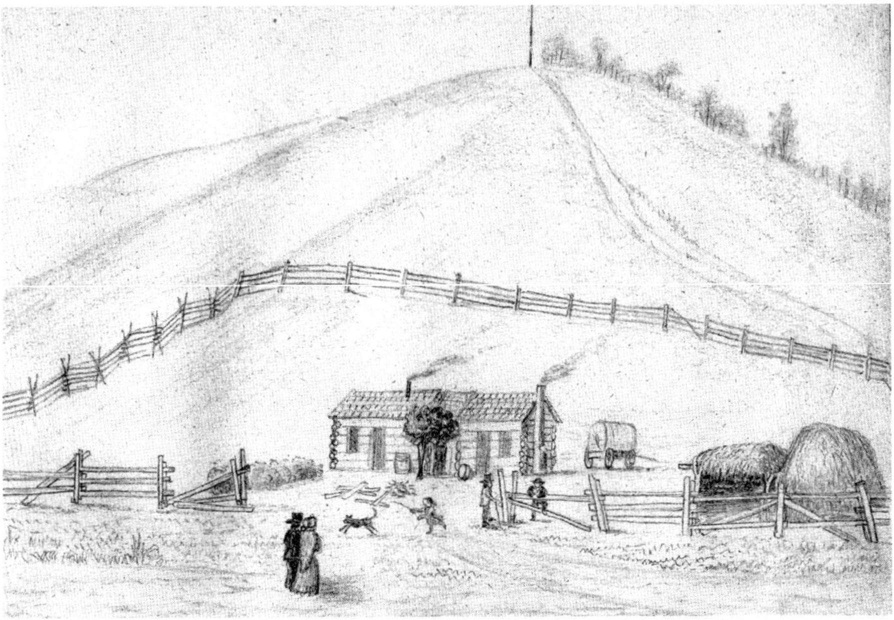

George Simons captured Orson Hyde's home. Typical of the earliest structures built in the area, it was made of logs.

In 1849, Orson Hyde established the *Frontier Guardian*, the area's first newspaper. Since Hyde was one of the Council of Twelve, his paper was considered the Organ of the Saints. The Mormon settlement flourished and boasted many businesses, tailors, blacksmiths and forges, mercantile stores, rope makers, gold and silversmiths, jewelers, watchmaker repair shops, shoe and clothing stores, grocers, dentists, doctors, outfitters for travels west, daguerreian likeness studios and the *Frontier Guardian* newspaper. In December 1849, Orson Hyde erected a log building he named Beebee Hall to be used as a music hall for dances and entertainment. The first non-Mormon business opened in June 1848. Donnell & Stutsman was located on Madison (First Street). Mr. Stutsman married and built the first frame house and frame business in town. Mr. Voorhis came from St. Louis, Missouri, on August 17, 1848, partnering with Eddy & Jameson & Co., located near where the First Methodist Episcopal Church would be built.

Mormon elder Almon W. Babbitt arrived in 1850 and decided to settle in Kanesville as opposed to heading west to Utah. He opened a newspaper—the *Weekly Western Bugle*—in opposition to the *Frontier Guardian*, though it was still a Mormon publication. His newspaper office sat on the north side of what is today Broadway.

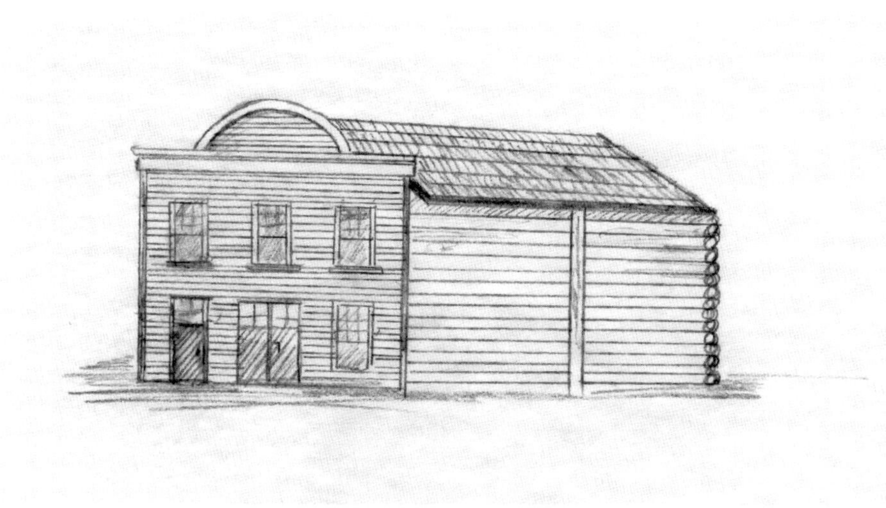

The weatherboard façade of Beebee Hall built by Orson Hyde was located on the east end Broadway in the 200 block of Broadway by Park.

For two years, everything was in the control of the Mormons. They didn't build any jails, for there wasn't the need for them. Also, there wasn't any alcohol allowed, as one of the tenets of the Mormon faith is temperance. The Latter-day Saints lived peacefully among themselves.

That gentle peace was not to last.

In 1849, everything changed for the secluded settlement. The discovery of gold at Sutter's Mill in California enflamed the nation with gold fever. All those seeking to make their fortunes in the gold fields passed along the route to the west the Mormons had established. This influx of gold seekers changed Kanesville irrevocably. Flagrant gambling and liquor interests blossomed. All manner of low-life speculators, gamblers and opportunists—men seeking an easy buck, men of all the worst sorts, of every calling and persuasion—flooded the area. The quiet outpost of Kanesville became a conduit to the dreams of wealth to be made in the western gold fields in California, Colorado and Montana.

With this flood of rough, unsavory men also came the camp follower plying her wares, for these men didn't bring wives or children. These men were not the sort to want to establish churches and schools. They lived hard, played hard, drank hard and whored with the available soiled doves who had washed up on the shores of the Missouri River after them.

Long lines of migrant trains wended their ways across the prairie, along the Mormon Trail, in 1849, a class of men wholly different from

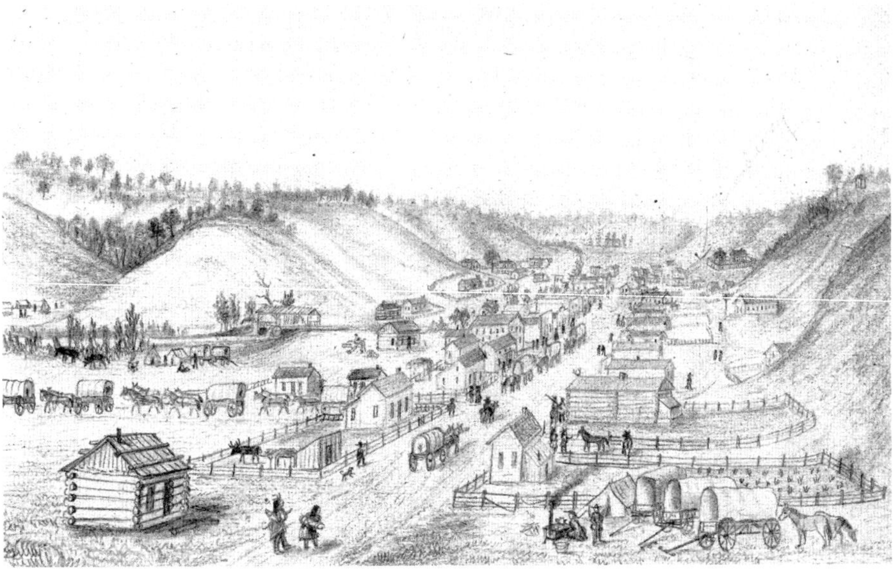

George Simons's drawings record the growth of the settlement to a town as the influx of fortune hunters flooded the area.

the peaceful Mormons—lawyers who had thrown away their briefs in disgust when the marvelous and fascinating tales of untold wealth just for the taking circulated.

Gamblers and blacklegs, farmers and mechanics all poured into Kanesville, transforming it completely. These men had left families behind as they succumbed to the gold fields' lure. They were easy to spot amid the population. The rough garb of the frontiers reduced all of the newcomers to one common level. They shared a common goal: risking it all in a dangerous leap of faith to wealth.

Women who crossed the plains possessed hardiness and were usually of a class whose life adventures and virtues did not include the inimitable charms of purity and chastity. The soiled doves plied their tawdry trade among the stream of frontiersmen heading west.

There were other profits to be made off the influx of hard-living, disorderly men. Selling liquor became the most lucrative business in town, second only to gambling. Saloons, drinking places and gambling halls opened wherever a shelter could be obtained under roof or canvas.

Not all the men who came to Kanesville at this time were among the lowest form of life. Some came seeing another sort of opportunity from the hard-scrabble risk of the gold fields and settled down, opening shops

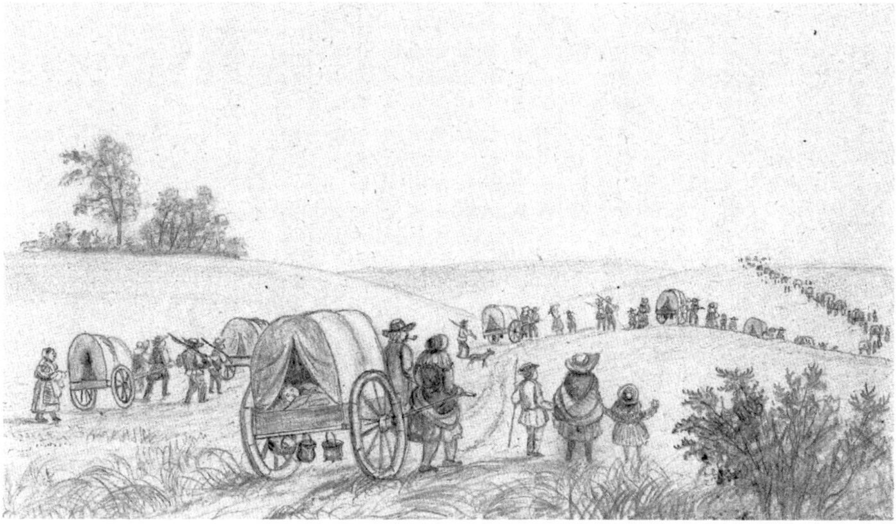

Kanesville was a portal for thousands of people. When Brigham Young called all the saints home, many utilized hand carts on the long trek west.

that catered to people traveling west. They brought their families soon after. They decided to stay and strike out for a different dream than originally planned. Some of these men would take the reins of government and help to build the small settlement into a city that they took great pride in re-creating.

By 1850, a steady stream of humanity was passing through Kanesville each season.

Mormon control concluded, and with it Mormon law and order came to an end. In 1852, Brigham Young sent out instructions for the last of his flock to come to their utopia on the Great Salt Lake in Utah. Businesses, houses and land went up for sale preceding the exodus. What did not sell was abandoned. They took what they could in their wagons and made their way to their new chosen home. At this time, about 2,500 Mormons migrated west, save for a few who remained behind to continue their businesses. Mr. Babbitt was one who remained and took over the *Frontier Guardian*, incorporating it into the *Western Bugle* and acquiring all the equipment left behind.

Once again, the settlement was almost deserted.

Some eight or nine hundred people remained. However, their numbers were greatly reduced when an outbreak of cholera reduced the remaining population to about five hundred souls. These men and women inherited the stewardship of Kanesville. What they made of it would have an impact on the future of the area.

III
CHANGING HANDS

A gorge, partly clothed in timber widened out from the east toward the river. This became Broadway. Crossing almost at right angles, a street north–south which lay in a ravine, Hyde Street became Madison or First Street. A few log cabins dotted the slopes of the bluffs on either side of the Indian Creek valley through which Broadway extends. The Indian Creek swelled to a torrent by summer rains or winter snow coiled sluggishly in a narrow channel around the base of the northern slope. Greater numbers of log houses and tents constituting the town were on Madison Street (First Street) and until only a few years ago many log houses kept their places as the surrounding area improved.
—unidentified memoirs, 1880s

Once the majority of Mormons had departed, public sentiment opposed retaining the Mormon origins of the city. On January 19, 1853, the name of Kanesville was changed to Council Bluffs City, and incorporation was authorized by special charter on January 24 of that same year. They also replaced the designations of the Mormon streets.

Main was renamed Broadway, Hyde Street became Madison Street, Race became South Washington and Market, though little more than a path, became Park. Even these changes did not last. On June 18, 1880, more changes were made to street names throughout Council Bluffs. Streets would run north to south, and avenues would run east to west. Madison became First Street; Market became Second Street; Bond, Third Street; Bancroft, Fourth Street; Main, Fifth; Center, Sixth; Marcy, Seventh; Baldwin, Eighth;

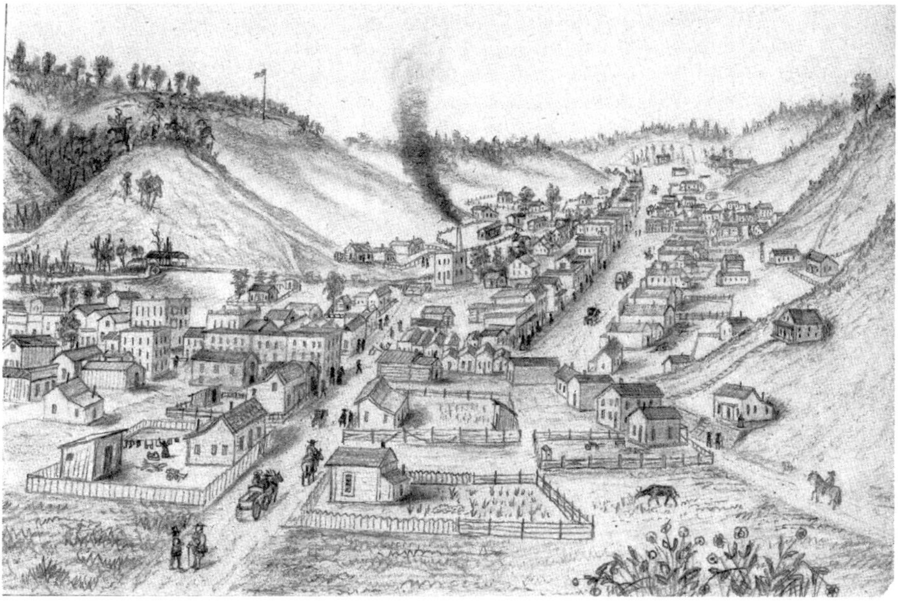

This George Simons sketch of 1858 shows a larger city. The mill on Indian Creek pumps out smoke, and houses and businesses line the streets.

Chestnut, Ninth; Court, First Avenue; Clay, Second Avenue; Fillmore, Third; Curtis, Fourth; Buckingham and Dodge Streets, Fifth; Ramsey, Sixth; Wall, Seventh; and so on through town. In 1853, there were fewer streets to rename.

The waves of people traveling west still washed up on the shores of Council Bluffs City. Of these travelers, some chose to stay and open businesses, seeing a better opportunity in providing the migrants with what they needed on their journey as opposed to taking the risk of hitting it big or going bust in the gold fields.

One of those arriving had a lasting effect on the town. Too late for the spring migration of 1850, Mr. Christopher O. Mynster, along with his wife and children, arrived from Denmark via St. Louis. It was too late in the season to make the trek west to the gold fields. Winter would set in before he made it to his destination, and all the wagon trains ceased operation, waiting for the spring to begin their journey. Mynster traded off his stock and supplies to one of the last of the Mormons heading west. He also traded for a property that still bears his name: heavily timbered bluff land that became known as Mynster Springs. In town, he purchased a large log building and property formally known as the Chadwick property on Hyde Street (Madison). This building was located three doors southeast of the *Frontier Guardian* printing office. As one peruses the advertisements of the era, it seems all points in town located themselves in relation to Mr. Hyde's printing office.

When Mynster opened the Washington Store, he advertised his new establishment in the *Frontier Guardian*, inviting the public to visit his shop. Another ad he ran a little later, dated August 6, 1851, announced that a supply of lime would be kept on hand at his store.

His wife, Mary, also ran an ad in the *Frontier Guardian* advertising her services for midwifery. She informed the public that she had received her training from the finest physicians in Denmark, and her certificate was countersigned by the American charge d'affairs. Their home was located at their two-story log building, also housing the Washington Store, on Hyde Street.

One of the dreaded diseases of the times was cholera. It is a painful infection of the intestines that causes severe dehydration; the victim wastes away until he inevitably dies. The symptoms begin two to five days after exposure. The disease is spread by an unsanitary water supply. In 1852, Mr. Mynster contracted cholera, and shortly thereafter, he died. His widow managed his estate, living for a time at the corner of First Street and Pierce. She built a fine home at Scott and Washington before moving out to their land near the Big Spring, where she built another home.

Their son, W.A. Mynster, married E. Adelia Platner, the daughter of Ira Platner. Mynster became a prominent, well-respected lawyer in town. He was of the opinion that the origins of the town were out by his property, Mynster Springs. He would dig in the earth and would occasionally find evidence of the former presence of whites and Indians, stone implements, pottery and other artifacts. He probably found the remnants of the of Hart's trapping station and trading post. Another account refers to a mound in that same area where once a building stood.

On this land, W.A. Mynster later built hatching ponds, as well as several ponds for breeding fish. There was always quite a market for fresh fish in town, especially in the saloons, which always offered a supply of shellfish that must have come up the river.

When Mary built her new home, according to legend, the two-story log building that had been the Washington Store was sold, and the infamous Ocean Wave saloon opened. However, I question whether this is actually the same property the Mynsters owned as the Washington Store.

THE LORE OF THE OCEAN WAVE

The location of the Ocean Wave is well accepted as being where the Methodist church now stands. In perusing the numerous advertisements placed in the *Frontier Guardian*, it appears that in November 1852, Harvey Kidney and Ira Platner partnered and announced the opening of the Ocean Wave, located in the building formally known as the United States Hotel fronting on the public square. Within the Wave, they fitted up a splendid ten-pin alley, rondo table and much more for patrons to enjoy. Ira Platner was listed as the proprietor of the United States Hotel. Harvey Kidney was listed as the owner of the Gem Saloon.

Between September 1852 and September 1853, Harvey Kidney advertised the Gem Saloon and restaurant. The Gem Saloon was located at 75 Broadway. In advertisements for the McMahon and Williams drugstore, they place their business on Hyde Street, the second door southeast of the United States Hotel and nearly opposite the *Frontier Guardian* office.

There is a peculiar little twist to the intertwining of men and business. In another advertisement in the *Frontier Guardian* on October 12, 1852, an announcement relates the hiring of a deputy by the Pottawattamie County sheriff. The sheriff's name was Ira Platner. In tracing his other advertisements, one unravels quite an interesting life. His first wife, with whom he had five children, died. He remarried Elizabeth S. Blair of Council Bluffs. On January 28, he was divorced and evidently remarried again, for in a will, some property was left to Ira and both his living wives. He was quite successful in real estate. He would buy land and build or improve the property. Perhaps he bought the land and building that Christopher and Maria Mynster once owned, and instead of a mercantile, he improved the property and opened the hotel that later became the Ocean Wave saloon.

Though there was no notice of his death in the *Nonpareil*, Ira Platner died in 1899. More information was revealed when his son was killed.

On September 5, 1905, a call came in to the police headquarters at Bryant and Vine Streets. Most of the personnel were out on other calls, so the wagon driver, Charles Platner, and jailer Thomas Sloane responded to the call. They chased the perpetrator up Oakland and behind a house, where he scaled a fence, hotly pursued by Platner and Sloane. Sloane scaled the fence after the man, discovered it was a nine-foot drop and was still holding on when Platner approached the same place. Shots rang out, and one of them hit Platner near the heart. He couldn't be saved and died within

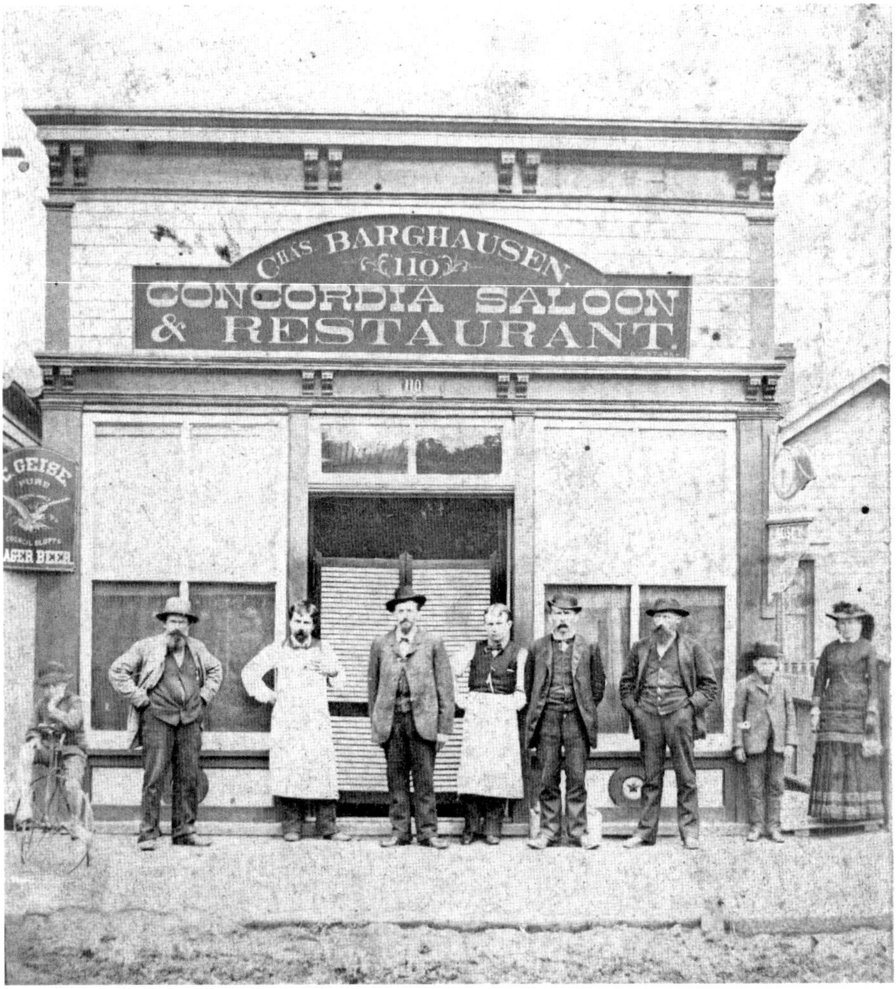

Charles Barghausen's saloon, indicative of the frame saloon buildings that sprang up everywhere when gambling was to be found on every sidewalk.

a few days. The information given about his family was interesting: he was born in 1856, the son of pioneer settler Ira Platner.

Council Bluffs City was not so large as to have two men by the name of Ira Platner. The pioneer Ira Platner, as mentioned earlier, was at one time Pottawattamie County sheriff, proprietor of the United States Hotel and even partners with Harvey Kidney in the Ocean Wave, the most notorious saloon in Council Bluffs history. He also owned a livery stable and later became well known at the Driving Park for his fine Thoroughbred stallions, horse racing and stud breeding. Among his horses were his fast runners Dawn of Day, Council Bluffs, Home Stretch, Long Stride and Ozark. The name Burhop's Hall was changed in the 1870s to Platner's Hall, and there is a Platner Street in the city.

For a reputation to spread across the nation in the 1850s, indeed, an establishment must have been quite a place. Of all the saloons that populated the streets, one particular saloon situated on Hyde Street in the center of the small town of Kanesville, on the western edge of Iowa, had a reputation that preceded it. Word traveled far and wide, and the place of business fully lived up to the sordid rumors. The Ocean Wave saloon became one of the most notorious saloons in the nation. Its raunchy, wide-open reputation traveled to even the most obscure mining camps on the Sacramento River.

The Ocean Wave was a two-story log and weatherboard building on a principal corner of town—what is today known as Broadway and First Street. At the time, the building was considered quite a magnificent structure in the heart of the business district. The addition of the weatherboarding was a step up from the other log buildings in town. The weatherboard was milled locally. Much of the cottonwood that grew along the creeks and river was harvested and milled into boards.

The Ocean Wave was remembered by contemporaries, who described it as having all the appointments and attractions of a place of its sort. At any hour of the night, the bright glare of lamps, fed with whale oil, blended with the dulcet notes of the fiddle quivering out over the soft summer air. It invited the homeless voyeur to its selfish, indulgent hospitality. Crowds of eager men—young, old and even in the middle of their lives—would throng through its door, precincts and tables. The men—booted, belted, spurred and armed—were well equipped for any emergency of frontier life. Men of nerve, audacity and bravado were admired, whether they exhibited their swagger in a hazardous stake at cards, drank more deeply of alcoholic beverages than their comrades or took offense for an injury, slur or affront, be it fancied or real. Every sort of gambling was to be found, and ladies of easy virtue could be had for a price.

The building jogged out far into the street so patrons could look out the length of the street, and of course, the Ocean Wave saloon could be seen from the far ends of the city like a beacon luring patrons to come experience the joys only such a place could offer. On summer evenings, tables were placed outside, as well as inside, to accommodate the crowds of men looking for a good time.

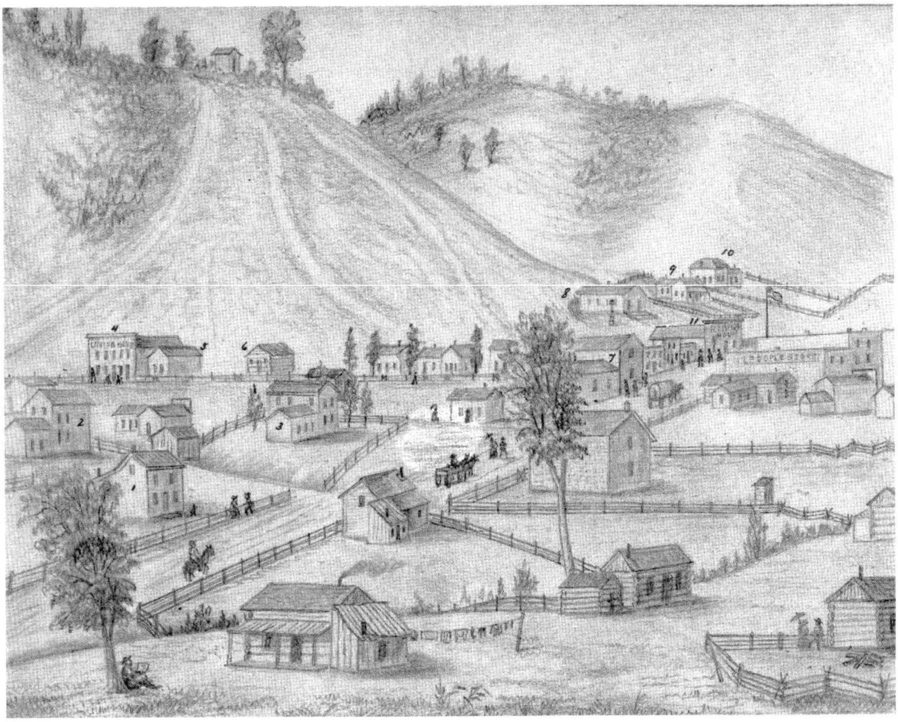

A George Simons view from the hill where the hospital stands. The Ocean Wave is number seven, and the Robinson House and Union House are also pictured.

In a twist of fate, young Henry De Long, born in 1834, came with the Mormons to Kanesville in 1846. He had been orphaned at age twelve. De Long attended school in a log house from 1846 to 1850, walking to the schoolhouse located three miles east of town. He would board near the school during its session. After graduating, De Long spent three years working at the Ocean Wave saloon, learning to become a gambler, until he completely changed direction and went into the service of God. In 1860, he was licensed to preach by the Methodist Episcopal Church. In 1870, he was appointed as a circuit rider for the western part of Pottawattamie County and Mills and Hanson Counties. The circuit rider was an itinerant preacher who traveled from one church to another along the circuit, or roads, in his district. Finally, in 1875, he settled permanently in Council Bluffs.

Violent storms kicking up across the plains were common. High winds, hail and torrential rains were part of the weather patterns that plague the area to this day. Tornados have inflicted havoc on the area for centuries. One such storm brewed over the small town of Kanesville, pinning one particular building in its sights. In 1861, the Ocean Wave saloon was struck by lightning and burned to the ground.

In yet another sardonic twist in the location's fate, Henry De Long, who had once worked in that saloon, bought the land where its charred embers had lain undisturbed for years. In 1866, De Long secured the lot where the infamous Ocean Wave once stood on the corner. The purchase price of the land was $250.

By 1868, the First Methodist Episcopal Church utilized the land and built a lofty new beautiful brick church on the site. Residents found this a fitting place to build a house of God dedicated to the salvation of souls, as opposed to the destruction that had occurred in the Ocean Wave from the debauchery of drinking, whoring and gambling. Before the Ocean Wave land was used to build the brick church, the Methodist Episcopal Church building sat on what today is Pierce Street, behind where the Ogden House would be built in the 1870s. The new Methodist Episcopal church was set back, no longer jutting out into the intersection so as to comply with the widening and straightening of Broadway. Henry De Long can also claim to be the first chaplain to the inmates in the jail; he would give sermons on Sundays, though they did tease him that it was seen as cruel and unusual punishment of prisoners. He was also appointed to

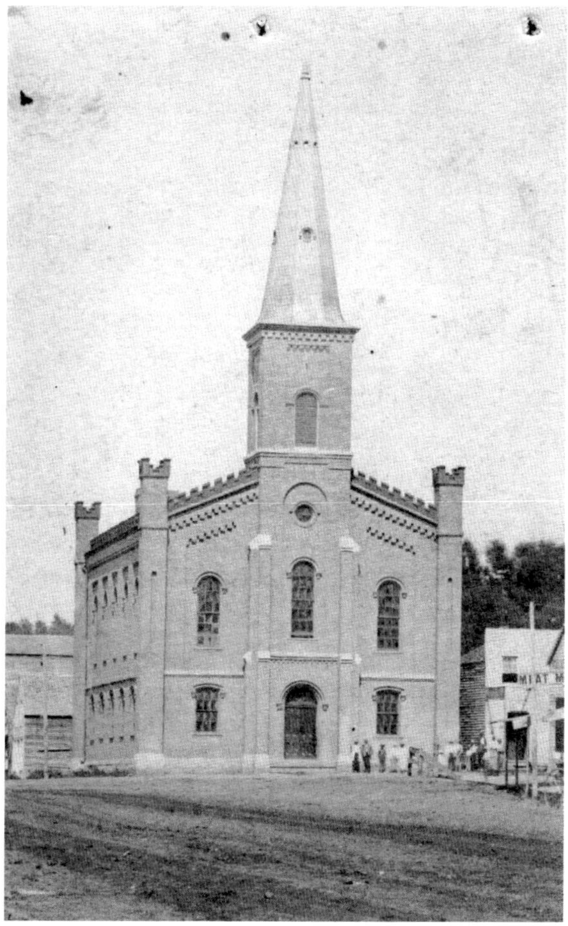

The First Methodist Episcopal Church replaced a house of sin with a house of God. It was later condemned for faulty foundations, and the current church was built.

be a parole officer and given offices in the courthouse, next to the clerk's office. This proved to be quite an excellent location, for hardly a day passed when he didn't unite some couple in the bonds of holy matrimony.

But the destruction of the Ocean Wave saloon did not end the availability of alcohol, gambling or soiled doves. Nearly every building along Broadway was a saloon or had a plentiful and varied selection of alcohol for sale. Ever since the influx of the first gold seekers, gambling devices were to be seen everywhere on every street, sidewalk, alleyway and vacant lot. On any Sunday, the entertainment consisted of horse races tearing down the middle of Broadway, kicking up dust and making it impossible to cross the street for fear of being trampled. Rowdy men screamed and cheered the horses on which they'd placed their bets in hopes of winning. Great sums of cash changed hands. For all this display of gambling and large, unsecured amounts of cash in tents and sheds, there were few attempts at robbery.

But not all the people who came to town sought only pleasure in the saloons, gambling places and sporting houses.

Uncle Bill Martin and Old Bill Powers had a unique partnership and method of sharing their profits. Every week or two—or as needed, depending on the success of their business venture—the men would travel together, taking the ferry across the Elkhorn River and bringing the money they had made with them, carried in a sack. They would place the sack of cash in Stutsman and Donnell's safe in Council Bluffs City. At the end of the season, the men would come to town, get the sacks out of the safe and pile them on the floor. Then, taking their place on the floor on either side of the pile, they would begin their ritual. If Martin took a gold piece of a certain denomination, so, too, would Powers take a gold piece of matching denomination. They would divide the cash up this way until the last and smallest coin had been divvied up between them. They'd learned this practice from the Native Americans and believed it was the only fair way to split their earnings.

The regular business of governance emerged as men who would change the course of local history came to town. In 1850, Mr. William Edmundson arrived to find about six hundred people living in the settlement of Council Bluffs City. He built a home near the lower end of Council Bluffs.

On April 5, 1851, Kanesville became the seat for Pottawattamie County. Judge James Sloan was chosen as judge of the Sixth District Court. Contemporaries described him as nervous, witty, Irish to the hilt and a professed Mormon, and his early court proceedings read like a caricature of judicial decorum. "To hell with the code of Iowa! I have the law in my head!" he would bellow out over his courtroom.

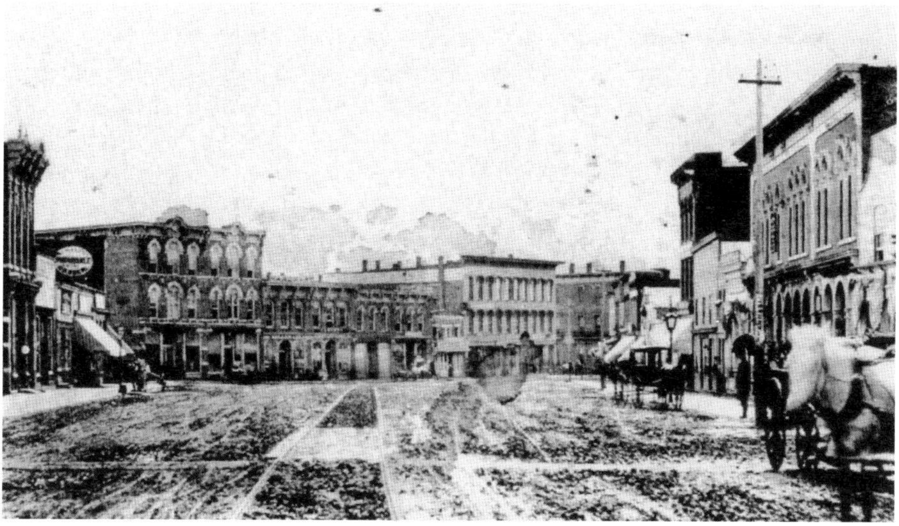

West Broadway and Fourth Street in 1876—trolley tracks in the street. The Keller and Bennett Block and other brick buildings stand beside the wooden structures.

Commerce in 1856 was conducted mainly on the river. In any given month of the season, twenty riverboats would arrive, offloading supplies before heading farther up the river, supplying settlements and traders along the way. On April 1, 1865, just north of Council Bluffs City, the riverboat *Bertrand* hit a snag in the Missouri River and sank into the muddy water. Though some of the cargo was salvaged, most was lost in the murky, muddy water. One hundred years later, the ship was discovered like a time capsule of 1865. The cargo is preserved in the museum at Desoto Bend.

The Western Stage Company ran the stagecoach line across the state. The roads were rutted trails, and travel was slow. The tri-weekly line ran four-horse coaches to and from Des Moines and another route to and from St. Joseph, Missouri. There was also a two-horse hack line to Sioux City, Iowa.

By 1852, Council Bluffs City had become the major outfitting center on the Missouri River for the migrant trail and did a lively steamboat trade. Later, as more gold was discovered in the West, new waves of gold seekers flooded through Council Bluffs City as they headed to Pike's Peak and the Colorado gold rush at Cherry Creek. But the problem of possession arose. Who owned what, and who held title to lands, became a muddied issue. Basically, the Mormons had been temporary squatters and never held title to the land; they never platted the town and subsequently abandoned the land and businesses they couldn't sell before heading west. There had been no taxes on squatters' interests. Official transfer of property was nearly nonexistent.

Samuel S. Bayless arrived from Virginia as many Mormons were selling their houses, businesses and other interests. He paid $250 for Mormon Henry Miller's squatter's claim. It consisted of four hundred prime acres right through the center of town. He held paper on his purchase that stated: "Jesus Christ and Latter Day Saints sell to Samuel Bayless." This document was signed by Orson Hyde.

Bayless proceeded to plat his midtown holdings and even plotted out a choice square of land and two other lots fronting on the square that were designated for the erection of a courthouse. However, the courthouse was never built on this land due to political differences between Samuel Bayless and other citizens. He was from Virginia and held views on the issue of slavery in opposition to most of his fellow citizens.

He also invested in a steam ferry in 1854, naming it the *Lizzy Bayless* for his daughter. It ferried people across the river into the growing town of Omaha, Nebraska. It cost fifty cents each way to go to Omaha via four-horse busses that ran in conjunction with the *Lizzy Bayless*.

Though there were many hotels already in use, the transient population of people traveling through Council Bluffs City prompted Mr. Bayless to build a finer hotel to meet the demand and attract a better class of clientele. In 1853, he built the Pacific House on Broadway, facing Pearl.

Bayless wasn't the only enterprising man in town. Benjamin Winchester opened a brick factory in 1852. Previously, erecting any building with brick would have meant purchasing the bricks downriver and having them shipped up the river on a steamboat. Fires were all too common and would rage through the dry, aging timber of the wooden structures. After the fire of 1854, people preferred to rebuild in brick provided by the local kiln.

Benedict Haag built the first brewery in western Iowa in 1855. Haag's Block was a three-story brick building located on Upper Broadway at the south side of Pierce, east of the Pierce Street School. Later, after Mr. Haag died, his widow remarried Mr. Charles Bock, and they changed the name to Bock's Beer Garden. The brewery closed in the mid-1880s.

The industry of pork packing began in the winter of 1859 and continued through the early part of 1860. Without refrigeration, pork could be processed only in the colder weather or it would quickly spoil. John Ross built a brick pork house on the north side of Buckingham Street, west of Indian Creek. By 1893, it had changed hands and was called the Stewart Packinghouse.

Indian Creek

Man likes to believe he can tame nature. Mankind has attempted more than once to tame the meanderings of Indian Creek. Usually, nature laughs at his attempts to change the course of a river.

In 1857, Indian Creek flowed east to west through the city, on the north side of Broadway, in a narrow, shallow, devious channel that looked more like the path of a drunkard weaving his way through town after imbibing a little too much liquid courage. The creek crossed North Main close to Broadway. When heavy rains fell, the creek would swell to a torrent on its way to the Missouri River.

The city fathers decided to straighten the channel of the creek. They dammed the stream above Market Street, conducting the water to a race on the north side of the creek, across from Washington Avenue and the City Mills. They dug a channel, straightening the course of the creek in the fall. However, as water coursed through, the soft, friable earth washed out between Benton and Center Streets for a length of three blocks, creating an ever-increasing chasm. The city now faced the problem of building bridges

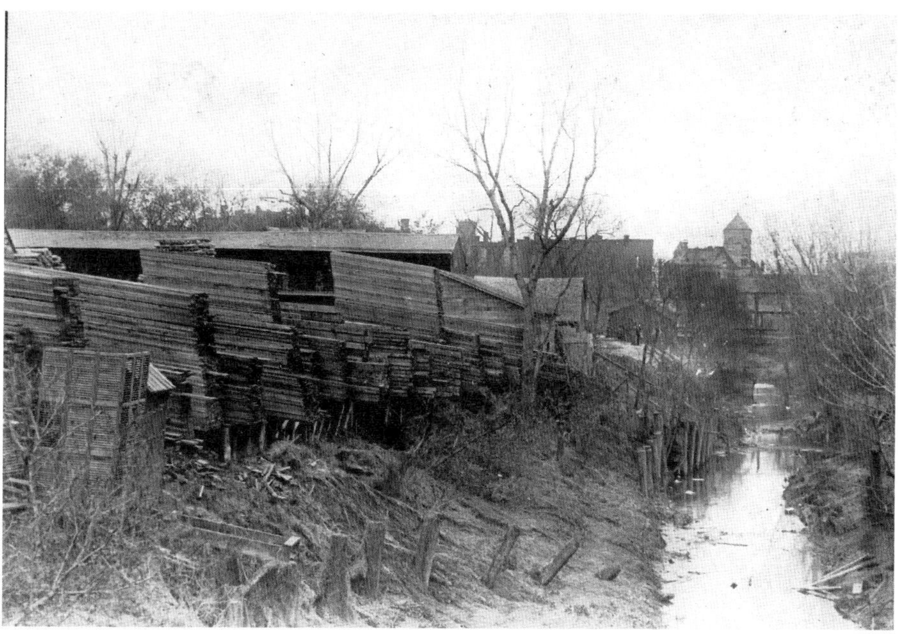

George Parks's lumberyard at Sixth and Broadway. When heavy rains swelled Indian Creek, the water carried off lumber. Did Quinn's lumberyard have similar issues?

that would endure across the new path of Indian Creek and the floods from heavy rains.

In 1893, there were thirteen bridges over Indian Creek.

The meandering of Indian Creek ended when, in 1934, a concrete ditch was built to carry the creek in the path that engineers chose. This concrete trough was constructed using federal grant money of $1.5 million. In other places, the creek was forced underground and into culverts to try to tame the unruly stream.

Just as they attempted to change the Indian Creek, so, too, had Broadway originally been a meandering path that needed reining in. Between First Street and Main Broadway was quite irregular. Many houses jutted out into the street, the worst offender being the Ocean Wave saloon. The city standardized the width of Broadway in 1856, making building owners pull back their structures to conform to the straightened roadway. The only building that made no change was the Ocean Wave.

In 1857, the streets were graded. Though still dirt and terribly muddy when it rained, they had been levelled. After the building of the original Ogden House, the level of the streets was raised. The enormous cornerstone was no longer so visible. It wasn't until 1884 that some of the principal streets were paved with Sioux Falls granite. Some lesser streets were paved with cedar blocks.

Indian Creek was not the only feature of nature to be assaulted by the civilizing hands of mankind. The Loess Hills were whittled away and utilized for raising and grading the streets in both Council Bluffs and Omaha.

The topography gave interesting names to these places. The Indian Creek Valley, above where the old Masonic temple sat at the junction of Fourth Street and Broadway and Washington Avenue, was originally called Miller's Hollow long after the name of the city had been changed. Park and Glen were known as Hangman's Hollow; Benton and Harrison were Duck Hollow. Broadway above Oak was referred to as Mud Hollow, and Franklin above Platner was called Irish Hollow for the number of Irish emigrants who camped there. Mud Hollow was where Lysander Babbitt built his home.

IV
LAW AND ORDER

Indian Creek, though only a crooked, devious, shallow brook was utilized and dammed above Market Street, the water carried north westward in a race which crossed Washington Avenue to the mill. Traces of the primitive waterway are still visible at several points, though the mill is gone. The last and only effort made to employ this fickle stream for any other purpose than drainage and sewerage.
—History of Pottawattamie County, *1883*

Once the Mormons' control slipped away with the influx of gold seekers passing through town, the need to establish a system of courts, jail and policing became necessary. In the early days, the settlement had only one marshal, no courthouse and no jail. Much of city business was conducted in places like Beebee Hall or other log shacks until someplace suitable could be procured.

There was no police force then, only the marshal. Dexter Bloomer commented that every available building was converted into a gambling and drinking hall. The need for law and order grew as the population swelled.

As the city established a government, the need for dedicated county and city buildings grew. For many years, the district court was held in rented rooms in the City Hotel.

Wood was scarce in the area, and buildings were often moved or repurposed; if a building was taken down, the materials were reused. Before the great departure of the Mormons, the tabernacle was disassembled and the logs utilized in other buildings.

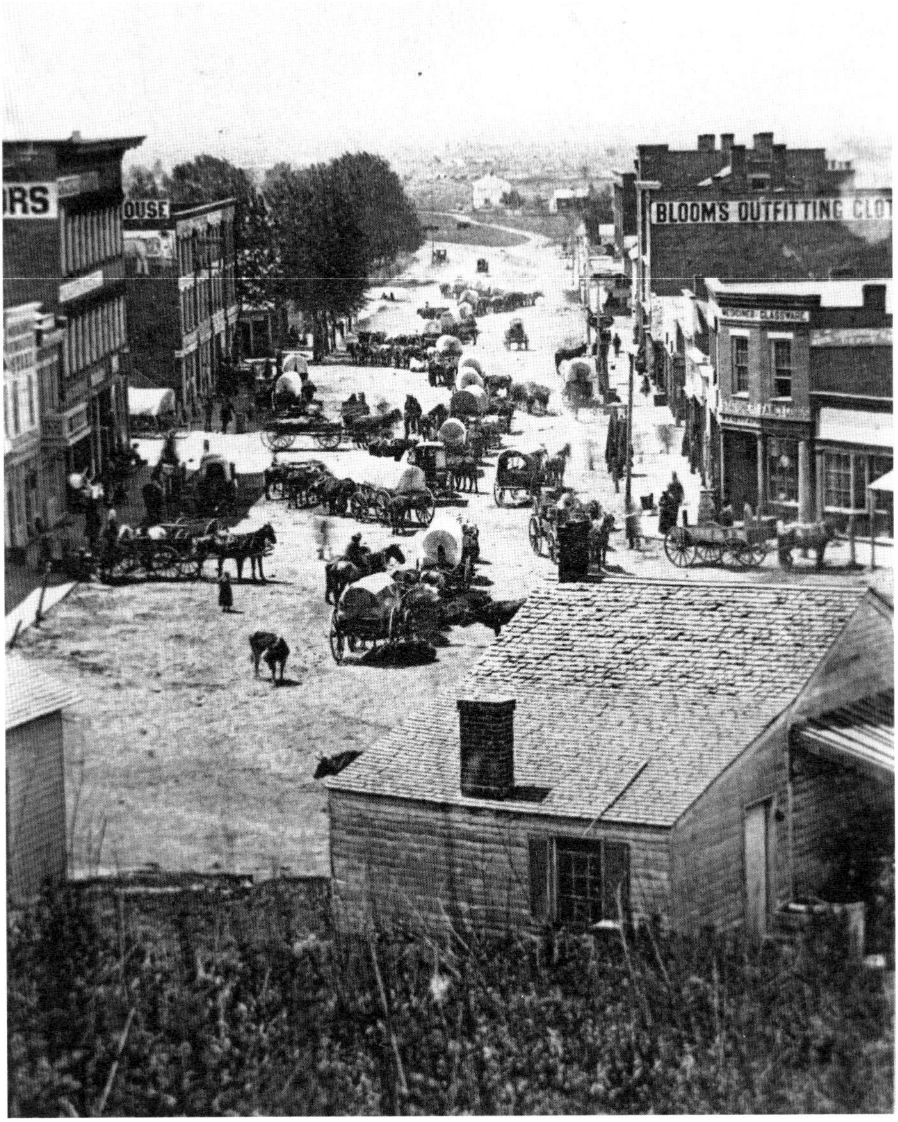

Broadway, circa 1864. The weatherboard building with the slanted roof in the foreground was the log post office built by the Mormons and the site of the first city council meeting.

When researching the history of the Pottawattamie County Courthouse, the county jail, city hall and the city jail, it becomes apparent immediately that they are all tightly interwoven in their growth, as they shared facilities, bought property from one another and sometimes went separate ways or at other times consolidated resources.

Every county and city takes pride in its buildings. The federal courthouse and post office, the county courthouses, city hall and jails represent a city's place in the greater scheme of things; they are meant to communicate a sense of permanence, power and authority. Over the years, Council Bluffs has expressed its growing pride and prominence through the buildings that serve the city and county.

Post Office and Federal Building

The first post office in the name of Kane was established by Brigham Young on January 17, 1848, in a log building on Hyde Street. It was known as the Johnson Emporium, with Joseph Johnson as proprietor. He kept a store and post office on the first floor, and the *Bugle* newspaper occupied the second floor.

The city needed new and modern facilities to meet the needs of the growing population. A grand edifice for the customhouse, post office and federal courts was erected. Soon, the post office became cramped, and a large addition was added.

The new courthouse was dedicated on March 7, 1888, with a grand banquet of six courses. The *Nonpareil* crowed about the building in its February 29, 1888 edition: "Without boasting it is the finest structure of its kind in the state. In size and finish, it rivals the capital at Des Moines. It is modern in architecture, in design and finish. It is a splendid temple of justice and we hope may answer the necessities of this county for many years to come."

The federal courthouse and post office at Sixth Street and West Broadway opened on September 7, 1888. The first floor was dedicated to the postal service and postmaster's offices. The second floor contained a U.S. federal courtroom and chambers for the federal judges and their retiring apartments, along with the marshal's and clerk's offices.

The third floor held offices for additional judges, the U.S. attorney, the board of pension examiners, the Internal Revenue collections offices and a library room. On the fourth floor, the custodian kept an office and supplies. Also on the fourth floor were some smaller courtrooms and jury rooms, reception rooms and sleeping and bathing apartments for railroad and postal clerks, plus reading and smoking apartments.

On the fifth floor were the attics and storage.

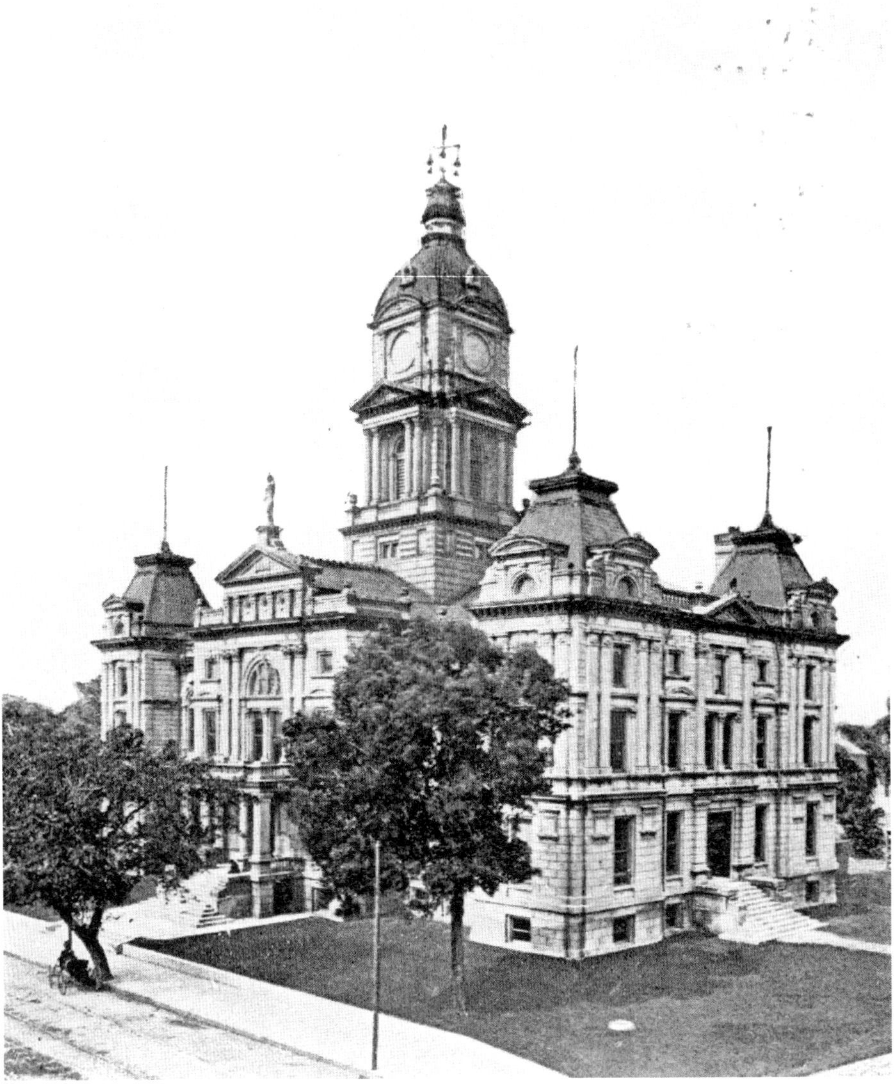

The Pottawattamie County Courthouse on a postcard. The building stood as a statement to the grandeur and importance of the city.

The building was constructed with Amherst stone from Ohio. Water was piped to each floor; there were open fireplaces, and ventilators kept the building cool in summer while steam heated it in winter. Gas fixtures were created expressly for this building by T.W. Wilwarth & Co. of Chicago. Brussels carpets were used throughout the building, except for in the jury rooms. There was even a hydraulic elevator. The halls were decorated in

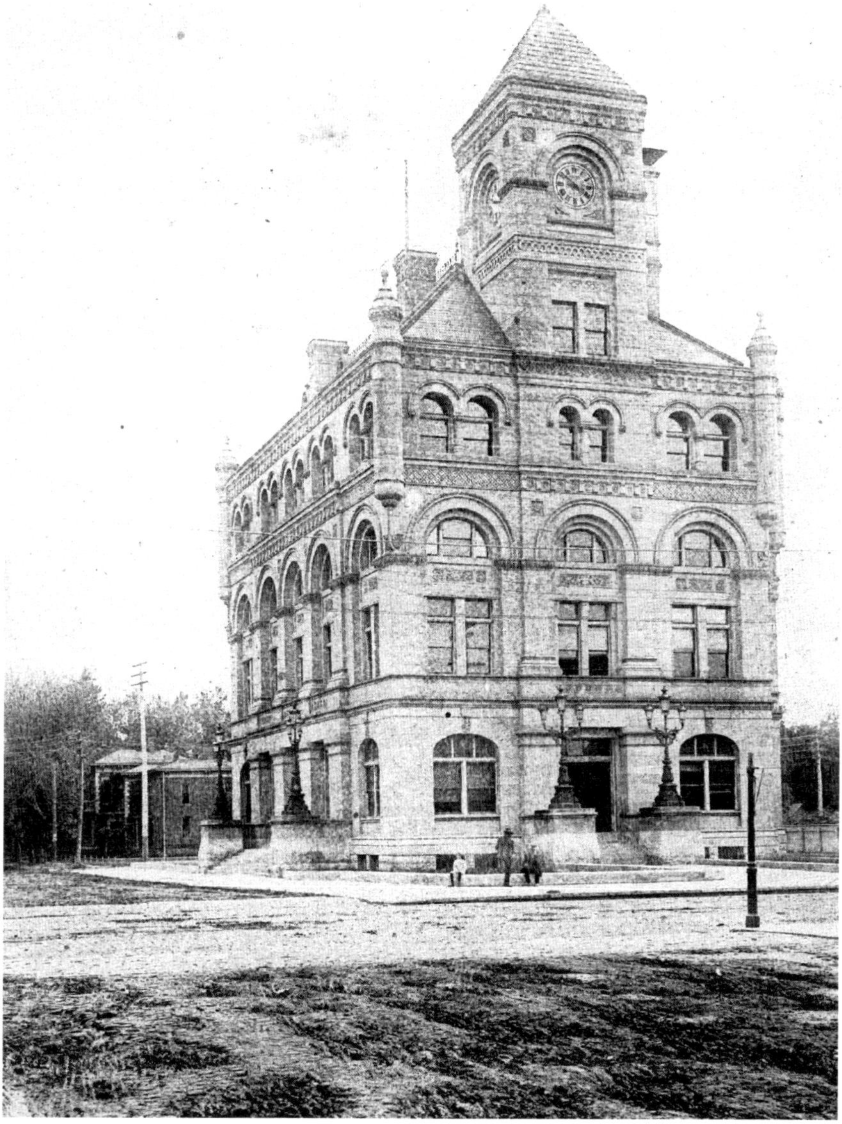

The 1885 newly completed post office and federal courthouse towers above its surroundings. Soon, the building would be expanded.

checked marble tiling, with oak wainscot finish and some carved details. There were seventeen Seth Thomas regulators for telling time. Traverse stairs were built at north end leading to the fourth floor, with a smaller staircase in the south end that began on the second floor and led up to the fifth floor, where an iron spiral staircase led to the roof and tower.

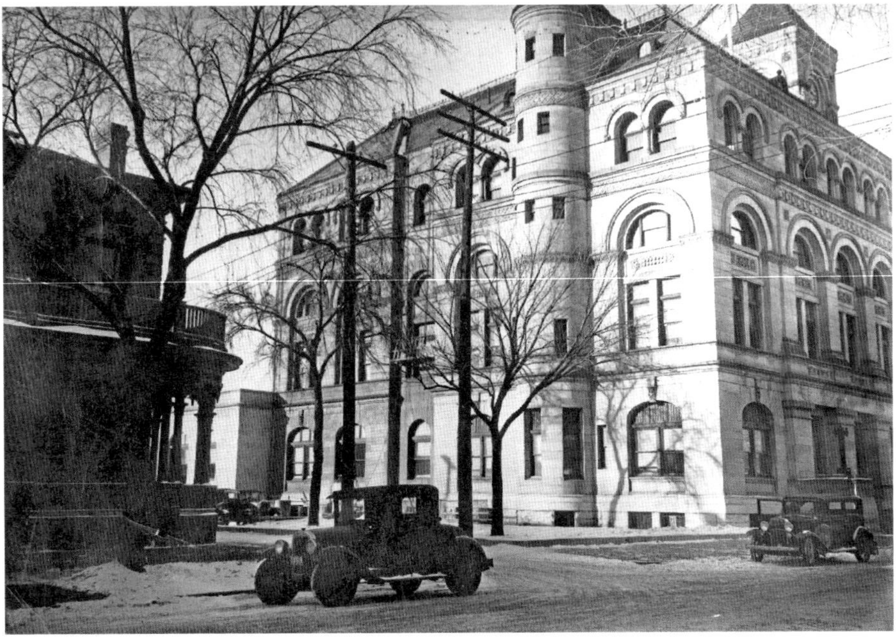

A 1920s winter photo of the newly expanded post office and federal courthouse.

The basement contained the heat and ventilating apparatuses, storage, closets and janitorial supplies. There were two fronts to the building, with the principal façade on Sixth Street and the other on Broadway.

It was described at the time as massive, grand, wide and majestic. This courthouse sent a message that this city was important and confident.

The courtroom and post office would soon prove to be too small, requiring an addition. In 1910, builders enlarged the courtroom and post office areas. While the post offices were being enlarged, the Merriam Block served as a temporary post office.

The enlarged courtrooms and post office area served for a time before they again faced the same issues: they were too crowded. Another post office addition was begun in the late 1940s. The City Auditorium, located at Washington and Bryant, was built in 1907 as a staging area for horticultural exhibitions. It was used by the postal service while the addition was being built. The post office was open from 8:00 a.m. to 8:00 p.m. on weekdays and Sunday from 10:00 a.m. to 11:00 a.m.

This massive federal building served the county for ninety-two years, until it was discovered that it was sinking at a rate of two inches a month. In an article on November 16, 1950, the *Nonpareil* addressed recent issues with

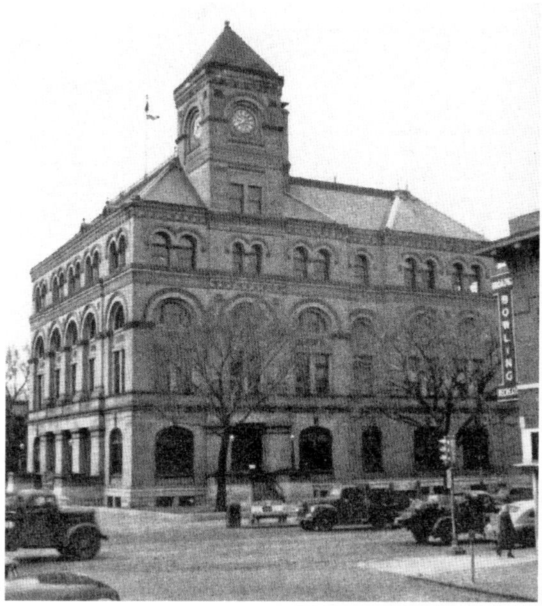

The post office began to have issues with the foundation. Engineers recommended that the building be taken down and replaced.

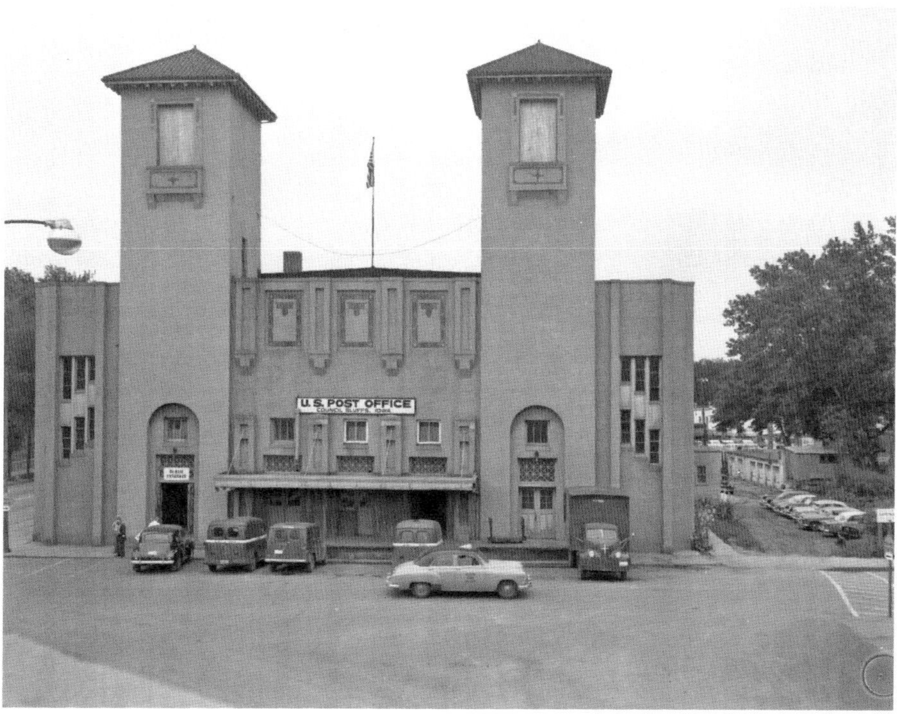

This 1948 photo displays the temporary quarters of the post office. The Auditorium would be razed a number of years later.

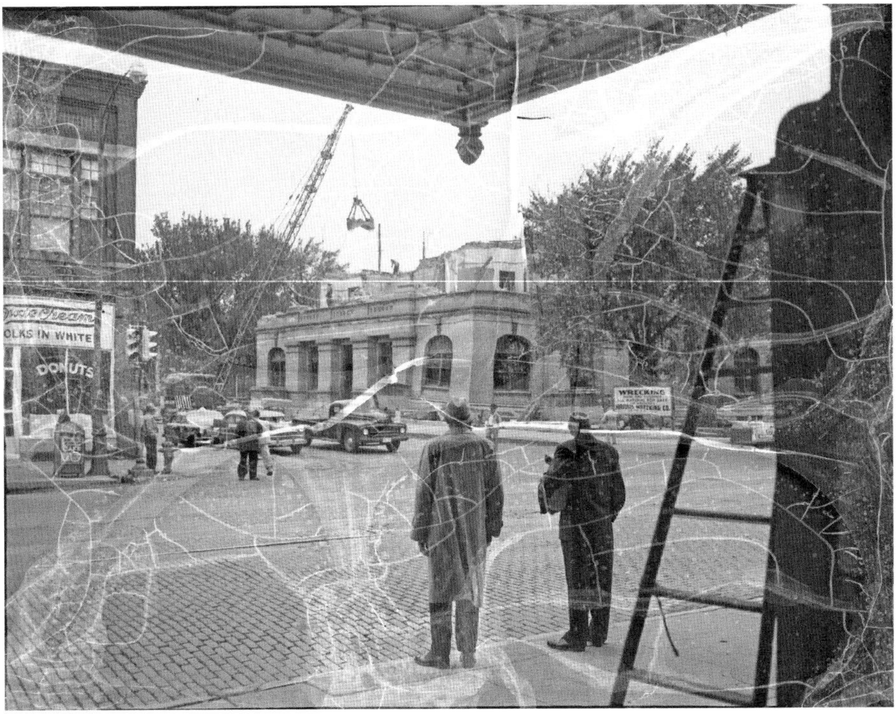

The razing of the post office building in the 1950s. This was the first of the grand official buildings to meet the wrecking ball.

the federal building. Evacuation and tear down were recommended after engineers discovered faulty wooden pilings below the building that were rotting away, compromising the stability of the entire structure.

In April 1951, the building was razed.

County Courthouse and Jail

The first courthouse the county established was described as a huge log building, constructed in 1849 and purchased by the county commissioners from the departing Mormon elder Orson Hyde. Before it became a courthouse, it had been used for assembly rooms and for a fancy dress ball. Located on South Hyde Street, later renamed First Street, it sat opposite of Platner Street. An advertisement in the June 1851 *Frontier Guardian* announced the purchase of the courthouse. E.M. Green, the clerk, provided

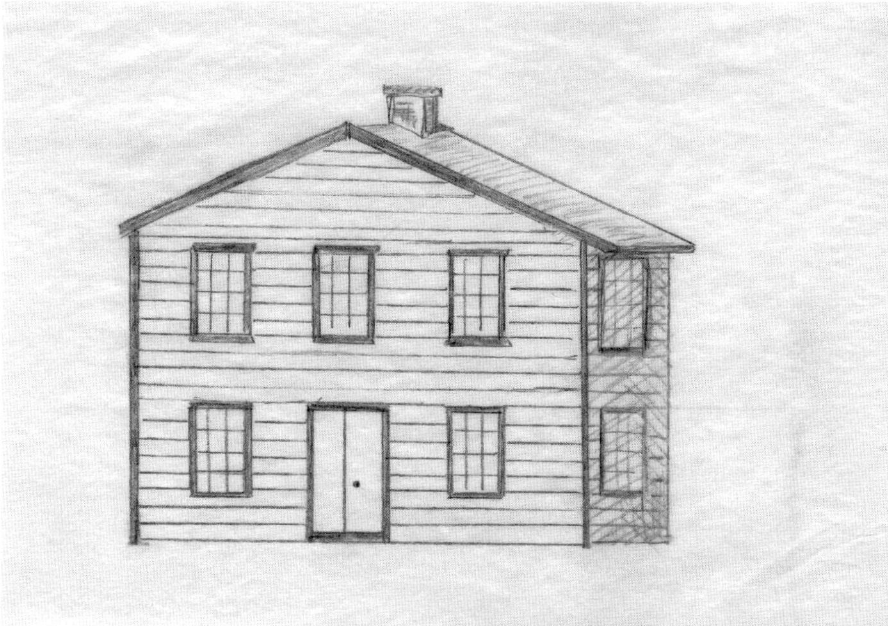

In 1851, county officials purchased Orson Hyde's Hall on Market Street for the county courthouse. The jail was placed next door.

office hours from 8:00 a.m. to 12:00 p.m. in the mornings and from 2:00 to 5:00 p.m. in the afternoons.

The courthouse also served as a school over the years. In newspapers, articles relate that in 1853, Mr. Brown taught school in the courthouse building. After the old log courthouse was abandoned, it was utilized as a school for many years until new school buildings replaced the old structure.

The need for a jail prompted swift action, coming hard on the heels of securing the courthouse. A calaboose committee was appointed to procure a house suitable to convert to a jail. The committee recommended a log house belonging to Alderman Jonathan Stutsman, located opposite Alderman Johnson's house. It would need repairs. Stutsman offered it free for one year. In 1849, the old house was moved to Vine and Market Streets. Under the watchful eye of Judge Frank Street, men nailed three-inch cottonwood planks, doubled, to cover the joints of the log structure underneath, and spikes were driven into the logs to prevent prisoners from sawing their way out. The building became known as the Cottonwood Jail. It was furnished with a bunk, a table and two chairs and had a wood-burning stove. The jail measured anywhere from twelve feet square to fourteen feet square,

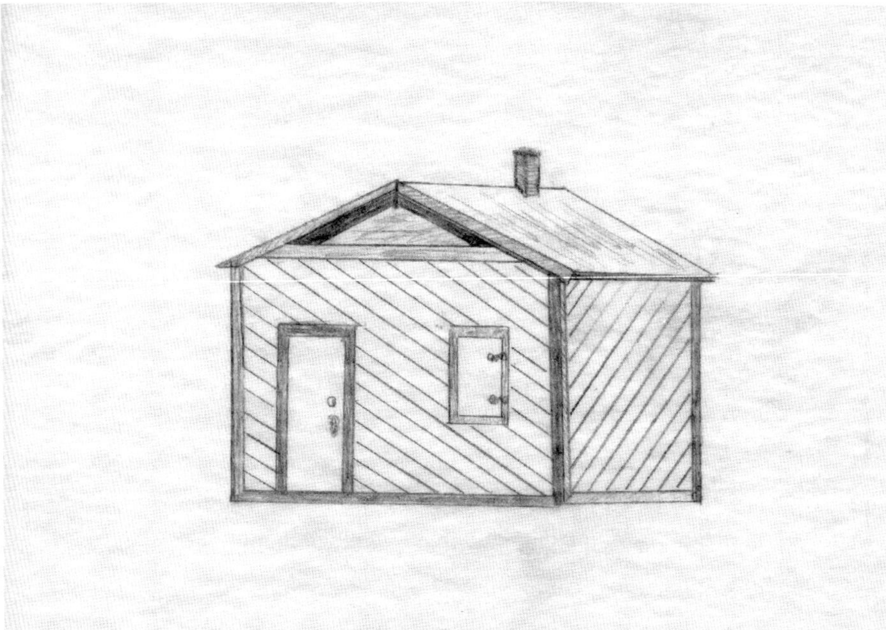

A cabin was refitted for the jail. Cottonwood weatherboards were added in double thickness over the log frame to prevent prisoners from sawing their way out.

depending on the source. Another description of the Cottonwood Jail gives the dimensions as eighteen feet square.

The log courthouse would no longer serve the growing city. It was antiquated. County offices located at Hyde's New Hall had become too cramped. In 1866, the county board purchased three lots at the corner of Pearl and Buckingham Streets for $3,500 for a new courthouse. Samuel Bayless had platted out and donated a city block to the town for the building of a courthouse. This land was not utilized. There were political differences between Mr. Bayless and other members of town. Bayless's sympathies as a southern colonial contributed to the city not utilizing the land.

By the close of 1868, the basement level of the new brick and stone courthouse had been completed. This lower level would contain the jail. The brick, two-story building was completed in 1868 at a cost of $50,000.

On April 26, 1872, Susan B. Anthony and Annie Savery came to town to lecture at the courthouse. The ladies were the guests of Mrs. Amelia Jenks Bloomer. The Bloomers came to Council Bluffs in 1855. Amelia Bloomer and Susan Anthony had been friends since the early 1850s. The lecture at the courthouse addressed the issue of women's suffrage and women's rights.

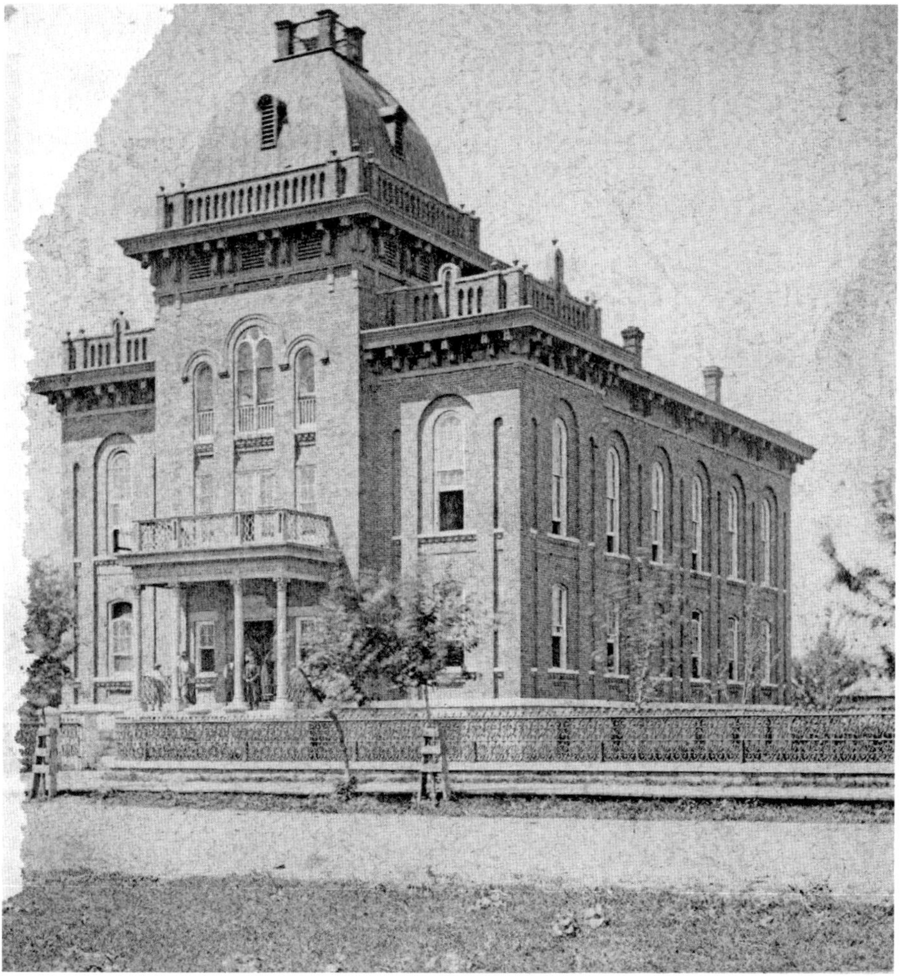

In 1866, lots were purchased at Pearl and Fifth Streets to build a brick courthouse. Completed in 1868, the structure housed a jail in the basement and offices and courtrooms above.

These were issues gaining great attention. Admission to the lecture was twenty-five cents.

Within seventeen years of building the courthouse, rumblings were heard claiming it was no longer fit as a courthouse and jail. The county had outgrown the courthouse and needed something larger. By 1884, a grand jury had been convened to look into the issues at the courthouse. The jury found the structure to be unfit; the foundations were failing. Immediate evacuation was ordered.

There were a number of reasons for the failing foundations. More than once, prisoners had burrowed their way out of the jail. One man dug a hole through the brick wall of his cell with a poker. In 1879, police arrested a group of tramps, placing them in the jail. Twenty men were placed in a ten- by fourteen-foot cell. The next morning, when police came to bring them to court, only a few remained. The men had burrowed through the wall, leaving a large, gaping hole in the stone brickwork. It was patched later that day.

In 1885, the old courthouse was razed, and the building of a new courthouse began, along with the building of a cutting-edge jail. The new courthouse was completed in February 1888. Costs for the courthouse amounted to $165,000, plus $10,000 for furnishings.

In December 1972, the *Nonpareil* reported that the eighty-seven-year-old courthouse was sinking at a rate of two inches a month, and it was declared unsafe. It was decided not to make any attempts to save the old building, as it lacked sufficient space for the current needs of the county.

On August 22, 1973, voters approved the $215 million project to build a new courthouse. The new brick, bunker-like courthouse was built behind the old one. The 1888 courthouse was torn down and replaced with a parking lot.

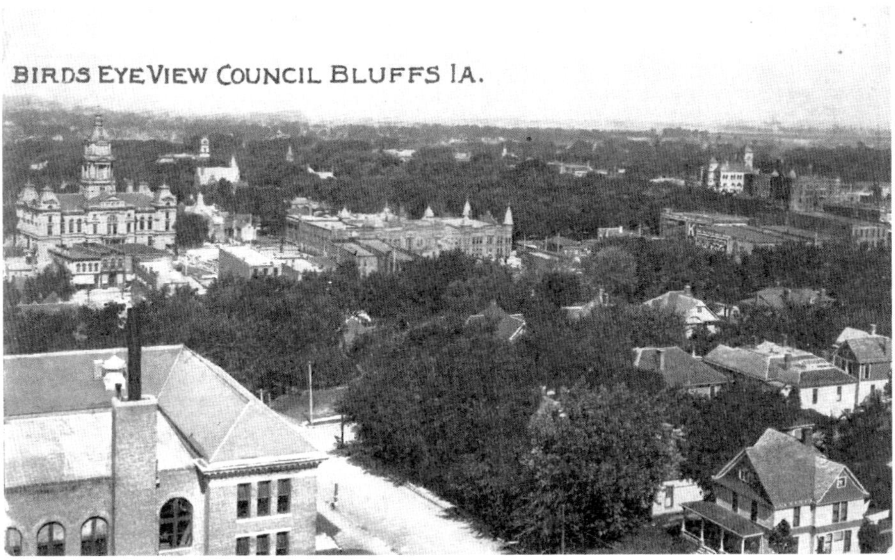

A postcard with a bird's-eye view of the county courthouse and the Squirrel Cage Jail next to it. At this time, the jail was painted white over the red brick.

Along with a new courthouse, a new jail was built next door, utilizing a revolutionary new design for the prison system. The unique design of the jail offered maximum security with minimal jailer attention. The jail featured a three-story drum, twenty-eight feet high and twenty-four feet in diameter, with ten cells per level. The jail revolved in a fixed metal cage with bars. This unique design was the invention of William Brown and B.F.H. Hough of Indianapolis, Indiana, with a patent issued on July 12, 1881. The Squirrel Cage Jail, as it was called, could be tended by one man turning the crank—one guard per level—to align the door of the cells. Sometimes the jail was referred to as the "Hotel de Guittar," for sheriff Theodore Guittar. In 1885, the jail was completed.

The rotation device was disabled in 1960, and the jail was finally closed in 1969. The unique Squirrel Cage Jail was on the chopping block and scheduled to be torn down. Because of the unique nature of the jail, the historical society bought it and preserved it as a museum in the 1970s. There are currently only a handful of these type of jails left in the nation, and the Council Bluffs jail is the only surviving three-story, rotary Squirrel Cage Jail.

City Hall and Jail

For years, the city had no dedicated building of its own. Rooms were rented in other buildings to administer the business of the city. For a time, rooms were rented in the City Hotel. By 1859, city offices were located in the Empire Block, a three-story brick building. The old building had served well, first as a bank and then as the county recorder's and treasurer's offices. However, in 1867, the building caught fire, and many of the records were destroyed. Fortunately, a good deal of them were saved, but the building was a total loss. In 1876, the city building was listed as being located at Middle Broadway and Glen. There is little information on this structure.

The first city jail mentioned in the records was founded in 1853 and located in a house on Jefferson Street. Prisoners were sometimes housed at the hotels in town. In January 1855, a prisoner being held on the third floor of the Pacific House managed to escape.

When the county built a new courthouse, it put the jail in the basement. On April 7, 1862, the city bought the old Cottonwood Jail from the county for $100. The building was moved to Market and Vine Streets.

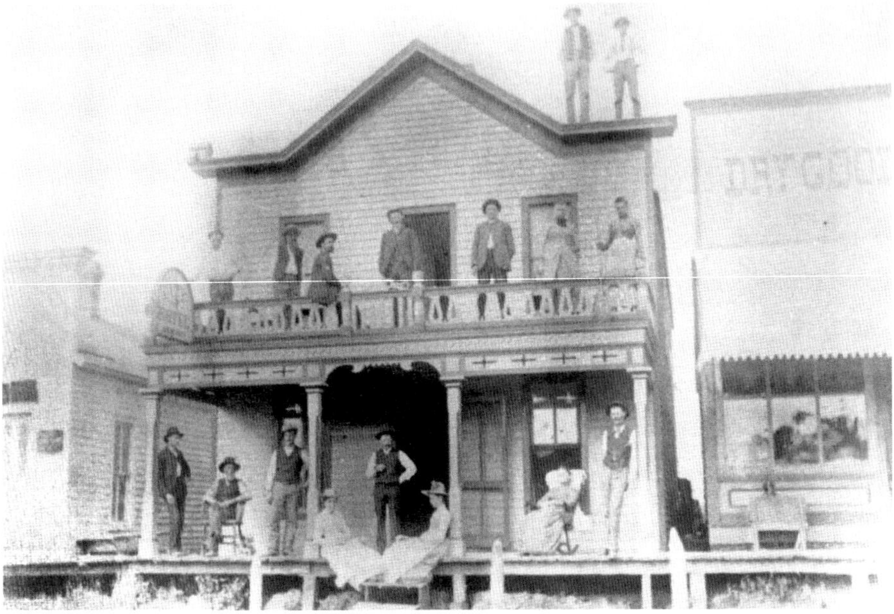

The City Hotel, located on Broadway, was a two-story wooden structure. The city rented rooms there to conduct business.

This jail was destroyed by fire on November 29, 1866, claiming a prisoner's life. It was believed the prisoner may have tried to set the fire to escape using some kindling for the heat stove. His cries were heard as the fire took hold; however, responders were unable to save him.

A new jail was built to replace it. An 1876 city directory lists a calaboose located in the City Building on Middle Broadway and Glen Avenue, at the corner.

In 1882, ground was obtained at Bryant and Vine Streets to build a new police station and jail. By 1883, new plans were being made for a city hall and jail on Bryant Street.

Finally, in 1884, the city moved into new quarters, to a building of its own on Bryant Street fronting on Pierce Street, with an engine house to store wagons and stables in the rear and a jail on one side. The old building the city had been using was ordered to be sold, and the land was used to widen Glen Avenue.

A series of issues began to arise concerning the Bryant Street station and jail. In 1872, an article in the *Nonpareil* despaired of the comparatively poor conditions afforded by the city hall building. In 1889, complaints stated that the Bryant Street jail was too small. In 1902, it was condemned but still continued to be used. Again in 1927, it was found unfit for human habitation.

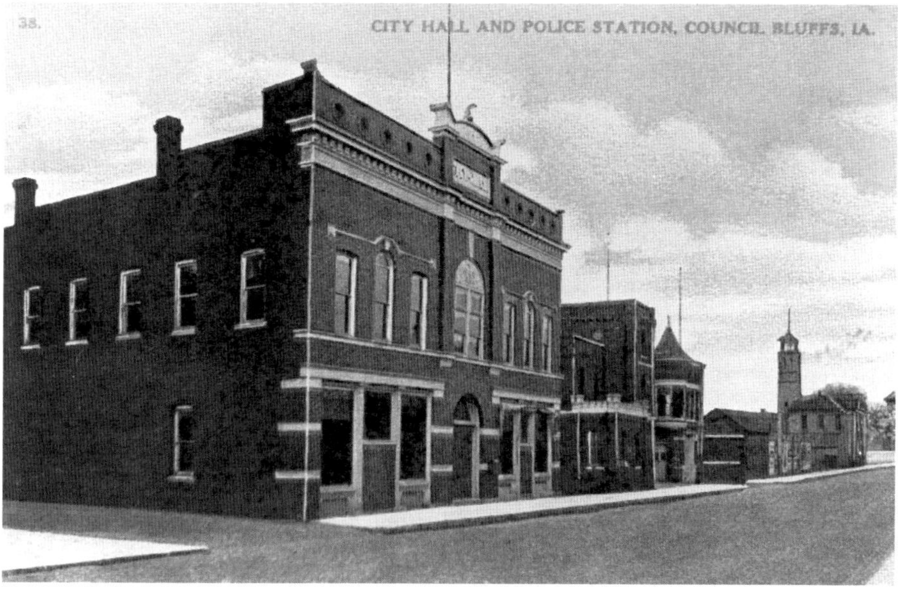

The police station and city hall moved into their new building at Bryant and Vine in 1884. It remained in use until 1940.

At last, in 1940, the Bryant Street station was abandoned and later razed. The new jail was located on the top floor of the new city hall at 209 Pearl Street. However, prisoners still managed to escape the penthouse jail. In 1977, the city jail was closed. The city and county joined together, agreeing that Pottawattamie County would take over housing prisoners in the county courthouse on the top floor. As the needs of the county grew, the jail space was needed for offices. The county built a new jail and offices for the Pottawattamie County Sheriff's Police out at Big Lake. The jail had 288 beds, as opposed to the old jail in the courthouse building, which had only 43 beds and twenty-two staff members.

Police Department

With the departure of the Mormons, crime became an issue, especially with the influx of transient men on their way west. Though there was still very little crime in town, steps were taken to ensure peace. On September 4, 1850, Sheriff Alexander McRae placed an advertisement in the *Frontier Guardian*. He asked the public for help in catching an escaped prisoner, charged with larceny. The prisoner broke out of the Pottawattamie County jail in Kanesville. A reward was offered for catching the thief. The prisoner, Mayberry Way, had escaped the jail in the evening. Another notice in the paper concerning crime appeared in 1851. The *Frontier Guardian* reported that someone had broken into Mynster's store and stolen boots and handkerchiefs.

Those who flooded into the area drastically changed how the town looked and how people acted. More than one article appeared in the newspapers of the day disparaging the changes. During the day, the streets—even the winding paths and sidewalks—in front of the log storehouses and canvas booths were appropriated by owners of gambling devices, and wild, lawless excitement was stimulated at every turn.

Young and old gambled; bearded men and mere striplings quarreled with one another over cards and drank deep from the same bottle. However, stealing was almost unheard of, and life was secure. For all the rabblerousing and wanton abandon of character, there remained a code of honesty. There was very little pilfering or stealing, and thousands of dollars in gambling money remained untouched. The cash sat unsecured in tents, log booths and cabins. There were no bolts or bars, nor was a watchman needed. For the most part, murder was rare, even in the heated passion of drunken quarrels. The men were armed, carrying guns, yet the taking of another's life or money was rare. A few instances did bring the anger of these men to the boiling point, and matters were handled with frontier justice.

N.T. Spoor became the first chief of police, appointed to deal with the rising level of frontier violence. While the Mormons controlled Kanesville, there had never been the need for police or even a jail. Mayor Cornelius Voorhis created the vigilante committee in 1853 to deal with the transient population, allowing the committee its own brand of justice. It took responsibility for a number of lynchings over the years. In 1853, murderers and robbers of fellow emigrants were lynched, and more followed. Spoor allowed the vigilantes to mete out their own punishments within their settlements. What is now Glen Avenue was called Hangman's Hollow, for there stood a sturdy tree where the miscreants were hanged.

Philip McGuire, a notorious character, infested Council Bluffs City with his lawlessness. On October 16, 1860, he was found hanging from a sturdy tree limb near the Fairview Cemetery. A note pinned to his body read, "Hung for all kinds of rascality." He had been in the Cottonwood Jail for stealing. The vigilante committee took him out and introduced him to Judge Lynch. Also in the jail at the same time was a man named Miller, a horse thief. He was found swinging from a tree on the east side of town.

Spoor did have his hands full; the licentiousness of the area forced the city council, in 1853, to order him to abate the numerous houses of prostitution in town. The soiled doves had arrived with the flood of gold seekers heading west. Some chose to stay. Business was prosperous for these "barques of frailty." Over the years, the city was accused by the *Nonpareil* of raiding vice districts and fining prostitutes whenever it needed a little cash.

Almost daily disturbances among the rowdy ruffians with a supreme fondness for liquor prompted the city to hire more policemen in 1856, and there came a call from the citizens to close down the grog shops. Fights, arguments, shootings and robberies all stemmed from the open licentious behavior on the streets and in saloons.

The police department was officially established on March 20, 1869, by city council ordinance, with the mayor as the designated head over the policemen and a chief of police. The department had offices in the City Building, located on Middle Broadway and Glen Avenue. In 1880, the police reported to the city recorder's office.

Police obtained their first patrol wagon in the 1880s. Marshal Farnan relates many of the issues early policemen faced in his 1910 article "My Apprenticeship as a Policeman." He stated that before they had a patrol wagon to transport criminals, police had to drag the offender to the police station if they couldn't commandeer a passing vehicle. Prisoners were conveyed by wheelbarrow, push cart, milk wagon and even an empty hearse returning from a funeral, with the policeman lying atop the prisoner until they got to the station. If the policeman had to pull and haul his prisoner through the streets, the public was sure to come out to observe. Even the rabble would come to heckle.

In the beginning, police were not required to wear uniforms. On June 1, 1880, police were required to dress in regular navy blue uniforms consisting of a cap, suit, belt, billy club and star. On the star were the words "CB Police No. --- [the badge number of the policeman]." The officer had to provide his uniform; the department provided the star and the billy club. Police worked two shifts: days from 5:00 a.m. to 7:00 p.m. and nights from 7:00 p.m. to 5:00 a.m.

In 1884, the police moved into their new building at Bryant and Vine. This building would serve until 1940, when it became uninhabitable. Over the years, they expanded the building as the needs of the city and police grew.

In 1900, more changes were made to the patrolmen's room and courtroom.

In 1886, three prisoners escaped from the jail, which was only two years old. They escaped by cutting through the rear wall of the jail. Police made the proper repairs within two weeks. Frank Guanella, marshal, asked for a new jail, pointing out that the current jail was too small, had poor sewerage and ventilation and was generally unfit. He requested more cells to hold adults separate from boys and to separate prisoners by the seriousness of their crimes and by sex. He felt it wasn't right to confine petty prisoners with abusive, insane or violent, drunken offenders. .

By 1890, the Council Bluffs Police Department had adopted a Metropolitan uniform for all police. Every officer was to provide himself with a uniform. Chief Wade Carey had many plans for the department. He wanted the uniforms to be distinctly different from the Marshal's Department. He also planned to have a second story of the jail building remodeled into offices for himself and into apartments for his force, thus freeing up room in the jail for the city marshal. He also wanted to start a detective bureau.

Prisoners at this time were often used as laborers, clearing roads, digging ditches and cleaning parks and streets.

In April 1896, the first black officer, Andrew Neeley, was appointed by Mayor Carson as a patrol driver.

By 1889, the police department had a patrol wagon, two horses to pull the patrol wagon and twenty-six call boxes. Between 1888 and 1889, the patrol wagon responded to 485 calls by police alarm and 275 calls by telephone. Arrests reported included 699 for intoxication, 400 for vagrancy, 257 for disturbing the peace and 9 for reckless driving.

Police were under the supervision of the mayor and were appointed positions. This meant a change of personnel after an election and especially after a change in the political affiliation of the mayor. A Republican mayor would appoint Republican policemen, and the same with a Democrat mayor.

Henry James was an exception. In 1898, he was offered the job of policeman at sixty dollars a month. For two years, he drove the patrol wagon. Since he was good with the horses, the newly elected mayor kept him on. The following two years, he was a jailer and had the distinction of driving the last of the horse-drawn paddy wagons before motorized vehicles replaced them. He worked until 1902.

The patrol wagon, horses and sewer department wagon all occupied the first floor of the police headquarters at Bryant and Vine. The police chief's office was upstairs, along with courtrooms. The jail was alongside the two-story building instead of in the basement. Bars were placed on the windows, and there was a jailer's room to keep an eye on the prisoners.

Often, police would gather the homeless into the jail for the night. This kindness was a last resort for those who were desperately poor with no way

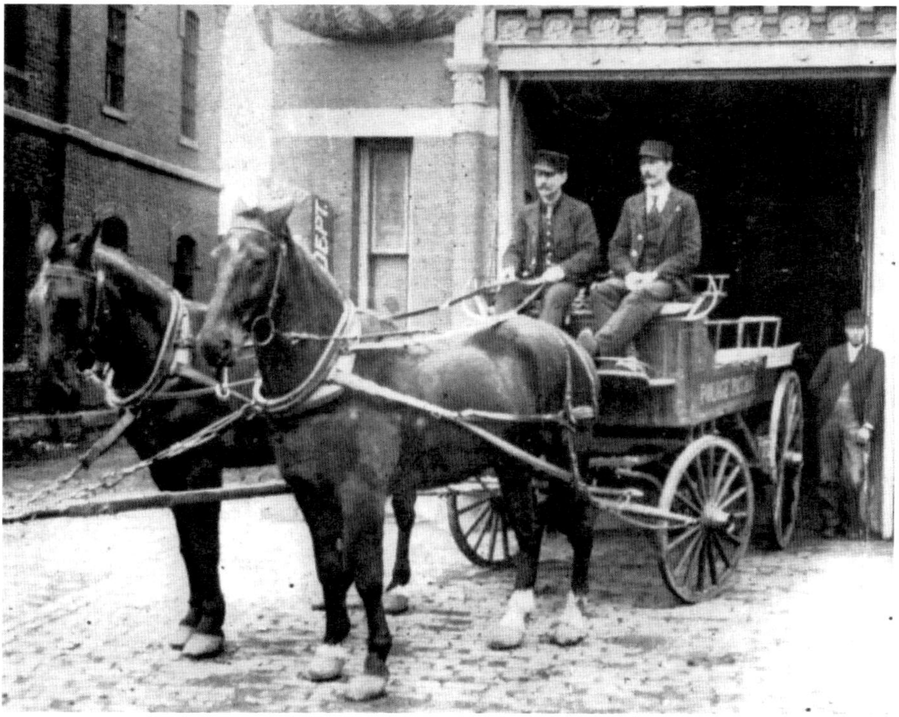

Henry James and Arthur Slack on the patrol wagon at the Bryant Street station, 1898. Charles Graves, foreman of the sewer department, stands in the doorway. *Courtesy CBPD.*

of supporting themselves. As a result, the jails were filthy and foul smelling and harbored communicable diseases. One of the police duties was to place quarantine signs on the houses of people with dreaded contagious diseases. On February 28, 1902, the sign needed to be displayed on the entire police department because a prisoner was diagnosed with smallpox. To keep this dreaded disease from spreading, the jail was under quarantine. Two officers volunteered to take the shifts until the problem had passed. The business of the police department moved back to the old offices over the patrol barn.

The *Nonpareil* wrote articles in 1902 disparaging the condition of the downtown area and the impression it must make on visitors. It mentioned the numerous old shacks lining Broadway in every possible state of dilapidation. This was not the only area to receive negative remarks. The downtown was changing, experiencing a building boom of a dozen new stores, warehouses and modern blocks. A grand jury visited the jails, both city and county, to inspect their conditions. While the Squirrel Cage Jail passed inspection, found to be in good sanitary condition, jury members were horrified by the conditions they discovered in the city jail at Bryant Street. This committee recommended that it be cleaned thoroughly if it was to continue in use for imprisoning or detaining people.

The facilities at the Bryant Street station became too old and crowded to accommodate the city hall, police and jail. A new Art Deco city hall was built between Main and Pearl, with an address of 209 Pearl Street. The new city hall, constructed by the Works Progress Administration (WPA), cost $300,000.

Between August 1 and 3, 1940, the police move from 26 Bryant Street to their new headquarters at 209 Pearl Street. Thirty-one men of the police department and city jail moved from Bryant and Vine, taking most of the furniture, files and equipment themselves. The old police station had been described as a "bed-bug-infested fire trap." Many of the men joked that the building would collapse if someone dared to peel the wallpaper off the walls.

It took them three days to move everything from the old station to the new. Even as they were moving out, calls continued to come into police headquarters. The old police station was officially abandoned at 4:30 p.m. on August 3, 1940.

As they moved, they discovered records that dated back to 1867. Sadly, they dumped two truckloads of these old records and hauled them away to be destroyed. During the next few weeks, WPA laborers began to tear down the old building and clear the land to be utilized as a public parking lot.

The new jail was placed on the top floor, and the new city hall had been occupied for only about half an hour before two young men were booked and housed in the jail. The jail utilized a "speakeasy"—a grilled metal inset into the door that allowed prisoners and police to speak and prevented the prisoners from spitting on their jailers. There were still jailbreaks; however, prisoners were not digging through the foundations and compromising the structural integrity of the building to effect their escapes. The ground floor on the police end of the building was where the police kept some of their vehicles.

The greatest changes came to the police department as technology changed. Throughout the 1920s, the beat cops were taken from the streets and given patrol cars as the city grew. Criminals also drove cars. Many times, they would have faster, more powerful cars than the police had, especially the bootleggers. The automobile was one facet of transformation that changed the interaction between the public and police. Another huge shift occurred with the use of the telephone and strategically placed call boxes. This meant that the public could communicate faster with police to alert them of any incident occurring. Next were police radios, which afforded easier communication.

By 1973, the police needed more room than the city hall provided. They moved into the newly completed Pottawattamie County Courthouse at 227 South Sixth Street along with the Pottawattamie County Sheriff's Police. However, this building soon became too small for the needs of the sheriff's police and City of Council Bluffs police. The sheriff's police built a new facility for their offices and a larger jail out by Big Lake. What had been the jail on the top floor of the courthouse was remodeled to house the county attorney's offices. The Council Bluffs Police used the building until they, too, found the space too small for efficient policing in a more modern and technological age with computers. The police department continues to evolve. In 2016, a bond passed allowing the Council Bluffs Police Department to build a new state-of-the-art headquarters dedicated to cutting-edge police work.

Fire Department

Fire has always been a terror to any village or city. The first buildings were constructed of logs, then of weatherboard and milled lumber and then of brick. All these structures were combustible. Indian Creek meandered through town and provided the source of water for the bucket brigades that fought fires until modern equipment could be purchased.

November 14, 1853, brought disaster to the downtown businesses when fire broke out, consuming many of the dry, wooden structures.

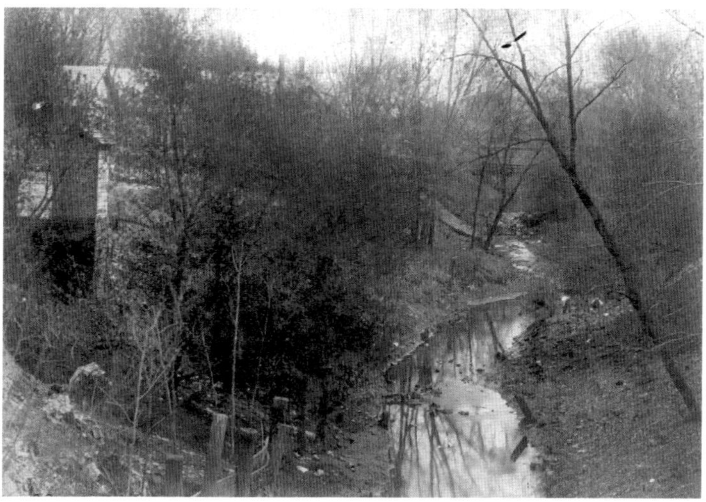

Indian Creek was the source of water for putting out fires utilizing a bucket brigade. Later, brick cisterns were built throughout the city.

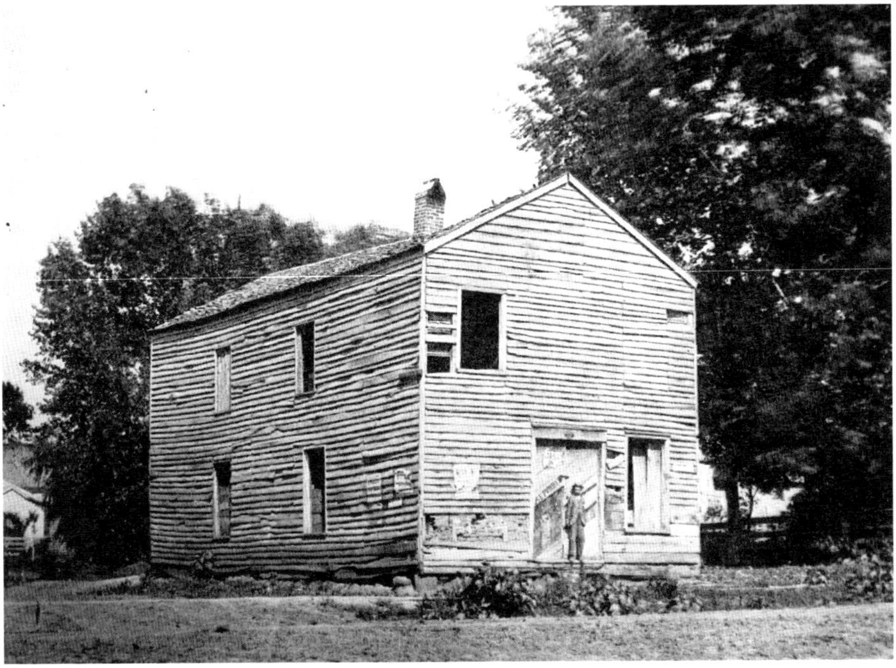

The aging IOOF Hall, made of wood weatherboards, was the sort of highly combustible building that once populated the business district.

About twenty-five business and houses on both sides of Broadway burned in two separate fires. The *Council Bluffs Bugle* was among the destroyed businesses. Not to be deterred for long, the buildings were rebuilt, this time in brick. By 1854, seventeen new buildings, many of them brick, were back in business. The newspaper was back up and running by November 1854. Exactly one year later, on November 14, 1854, fire destroyed the downtown.

On January 19, 1854, A.W. Babbitt received a disturbing letter from his wife concerning Council Bluffs City. He wrote a letter to the editor of the *Desert News*, a Mormon paper in Salt Lake City:

> *Last night mail brought me news that a large portion of the business part of Council Bluffs City has been destroyed by fire. The amount of property was very large, but the loss to the owners is uncertain not knowing what amount of insurance there was: but it is presumed that a small portion was insured, as the rates were very high, owing to the combustible materials of which the buildings were made.*

I've made an abstract from a letter from my wife on the subject.

On the night of November 11 [1853] *between 10 and 11 o'clock a fire broke out in the store of Tootle & Jackson and spread both ways, east and west, consuming every building until it reached Murphy's store.*

Such a sight my eyes never before beheld—in the space of about 30 minutes the whole block was in flames. You cannot conceive, neither can I describe the scene that took place. It seemed for a time, that the whole city was to be consumed. For miles, it was light as noonday, we could see men, women and children running in every direction, throwing water, tearing down houses and other buildings to stop the progress of the flames.

The Emporium buildings, including two printing offices (the Guardian *and the* Bugle*) together with the post office, were consumed with their contents. The stores of Stutsman and Donnell, Martin & Mason, Tootle & Jackson, Pegram & Bartlett, the saloon of Mitchel's, the whole emporium building; the store of Barrow & McLaughlin; Hawk & Co.; The Bluff House, with many other buildings, including the new dwelling of Mr. Stutsman, the bakery of Mitchell, the wagon shop; the blacksmith shop of Mr. J.E. Johnson; the stables and carriage houses connected with most of the buildings, were included. Very few of the contents were saved. It truly throws a gloom over the young city.*

From other letters of Messrs. Voorhis and McMahon the letter is fully corroborated; but yet, it seems that there is a determination on the part of the sufferers to rebuild with more substantial materials.

The rail road excitement is on the increase, and from all appearances Council Bluffs City is destined to become a point of considerable interest.

I am with high respect and consideration
Your ob't servant
A. W. Babbitt.

Firefighter and historian Cal Petersen related a concise history of the fire department in his book on the fires of Council Bluffs. The beginnings of the fire department can be traced back to 1853, after a devastating fire destroyed a great part of the business district. A hook and ladder with a bucket brigade drawing water from Indian Creek were all they had to fight fires.

On July 12, at Johnson & Orr's shop, the Rescue Engine and Hose Company were organized. It had a small hand engine and hose for its equipment. Good-natured competition stepped into the picture when, in August 1868, the Bluff City #2 was organized.

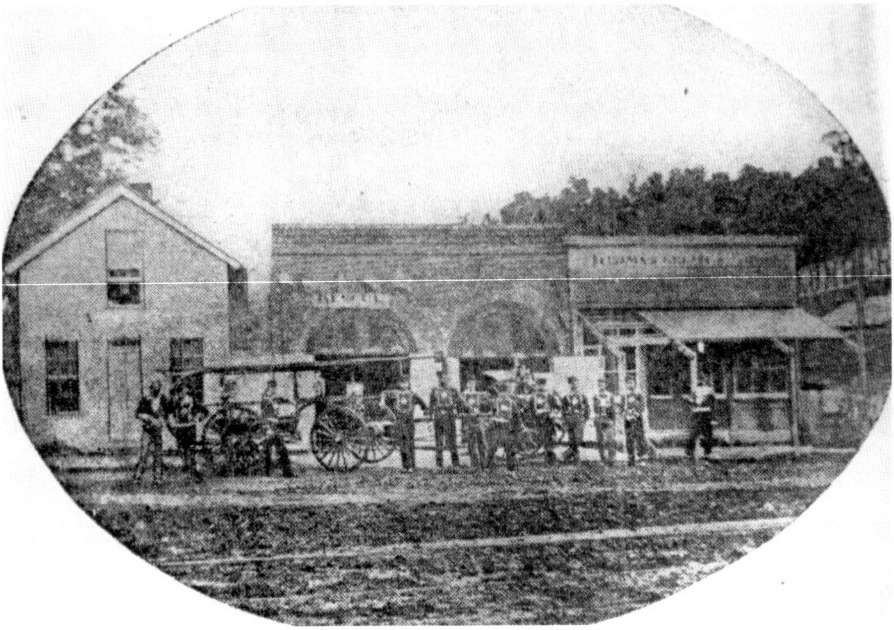

The volunteer fire department with its first firefighting equipment: a hook and ladder. *Courtesy Cal Petersen.*

On June 25, a special election was held to approve the purchase of the steam fire engine. The city ordered a steamer, horse and hose cart. The Rescue Engine and Hose Company had hoped to be awarded the steamer but didn't get it. The steamer arrived in September 1868 and was put to the test. A trial run was held at the Sixth Street bridge over Indian Creek.

Horses were a great addition to the department. Before horses were employed to pull the heavy firefighting equipment, it was up to the men to haul everything to the scene of a fire. These men would be weary upon arrival and in need of rest before they could fight alongside the other volunteers. Now, they trained the horses to get into harness quickly and pull the heavy equipment to the scene. The horses would be unhitched and taken to a safe distance, as fire is a terror to horses, and firemen didn't need them bolting still attached to the equipment.

In January 1869, seventy young Germans formed another firefighting unit: the Protection Hook and Ladder Company. Also, the Confidence Company formed but later changed its name to the Phoenix Hook and Ladder Company. This company was recognized by the city council and

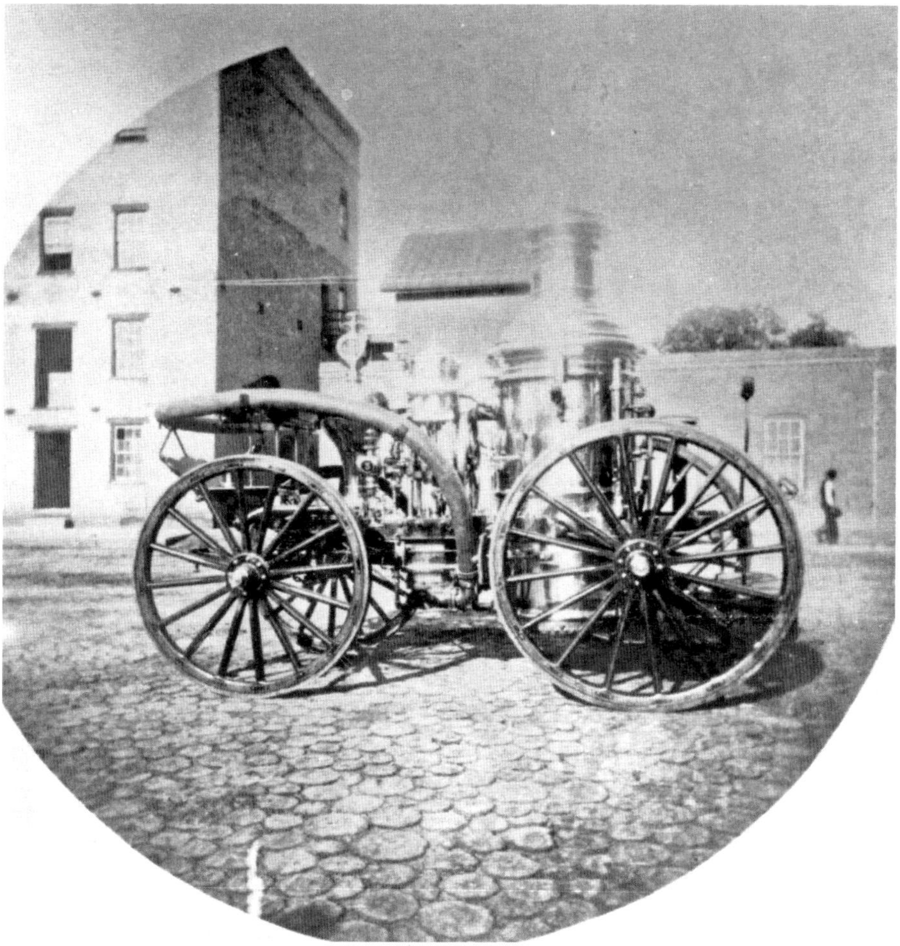

The 1885 steamer. It sits on a street paved with slices of cedar trees. Downtown streets were paved with brick. *Courtesy Cal Petersen.*

placed in charge of the truck. The Protection Hook and Ladder Company disbanded and blended into other volunteer firefighting units.

The hook and ladder was one of the most recognized pieces of firefighting equipment that any fire company possessed. The ladder would allow a fireman to climb up above a fire to douse the flames. The hook was employed to pull down a burning structure, hoping to keep the fire from spreading.

The city built a brick engine house at the corner of Pierce and Glen for the Bluff City Company. Neil Voorhis was the driver of the cart. Sam Morrison was given charge of the horses based on his experience as a stage driver. The horse was an immense beauty, weighing over 1,800 pounds. The horse was named Pat in honor of the fire chief. Pat served faithfully for many years. In his retirement from the fire department, he worked with the sewer department, pulling its wagons.

A second steamer was purchased in June 1880 and given a trial run on Upper Broadway at the Scott Street bridge. The steamer was powered by steam to pump the water—thus the name.

The first fireman's ball was given in 1869, with two hundred couples in attendance. It coincided with the laying of the cornerstone at the Ogden House and the arrival of the first Rock Island train in town.

By 1883, a professional fire department had replaced the volunteers, and newly laid water mains made the job of pumping water easier than bucket brigades.

The volatile nature of the wooden structures prompted a few people to construct their homes of brick. The first bricks had to be brought by steamship until a brickwork was established. The first brick home was built in 1853 by William C. James on the south side of Broadway, on the third lot west of Center Street (First Street). It consisted of one story.

The second brick home was built on the west side of Main Street, on the second lot south of Willow. The third brick building, a double residence, was erected on the west side of Bancroft, 350 feet south of the junction with Broadway. It was removed in 1878 as the city center expanded.

The fourth was also a single-story dwelling in brick, built by Mr. Stephen Carey on the southwest corner of Main and First Avenue. This was removed in 1882 for construction of the brick block by E.L. Shugart and the Citizen's Bank. On the adjoining lot of the double house stood a frame dwelling where General Grenville Dodge lived before the outbreak of the Civil War. It remained his home for the duration of the war. Businesses replaced their wooden buildings with brick structures.

Fire was a constant threat to the tinder-dry wooden buildings. On January 1, 1868, another devastating fire destroyed two rows of wooden buildings on the south side of Broadway and the east side junction with Bancroft Street (Fourth Street). Arson was suspected, though nothing could be proven. The county clerk's offices also burned, destroying many of the records but not all of them. Though arson caused the fire and certain people were suspected, no proof of their guilt could be found. At the time of this fire, Council Bluffs City still had no formal fire department and relied totally on volunteer firemen.

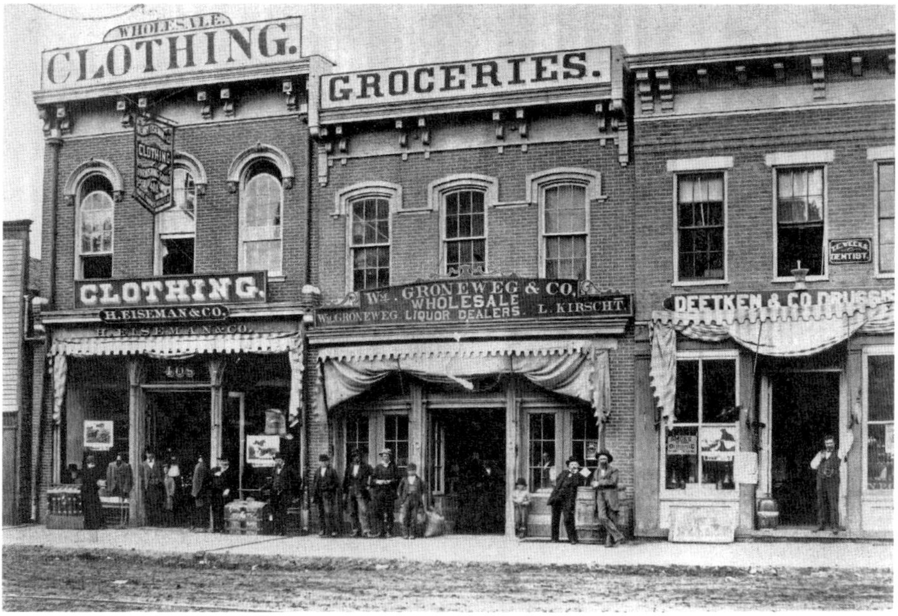

Eismen's wholesale clothing, William Gronewege & Co. wholesale liquors and Deetkin & Co. drugstore, with Mr. Weeks, a dentist, on the second floor.

Most of the fires occurred in the winter. The risk was always high with fireplaces, heat stoves, kerosene and whale oil lamps. On December 29, 1868, four buildings on Center (Sixth Street) caught fire. While the fire was being fought, the lines froze, and the soap and candle factory burned the following Saturday.

As of 1907, Council Bluffs could boast five well-equipped fire stations: 1) South Main Street and Eighth Avenue had a crew of four men, a hose wagon and team of horses; 2) West Broadway and Twentieth Street also had four men, a hose wagon and a team; 3) the station at the intersection of North Main and Bryant had five men, a combination wagon and the chief's wagon and teams; 4) Upper Broadway had a crew of six men, a hose wagon and a hook and ladder truck; and 5) Eighth Street and Nineteenth Avenue had three men, a chemical engine and a team.

The horses were trained to respond to the sound of the bell and to quickly move into position to be harnessed to the truck. The harness hung suspended for easier access and only needed to be unhooked from the supports and fastened to the horses. The men would drill to get their time as short as possible in hooking up the horses and equipment, as time has always been of the essence in responding to fire.

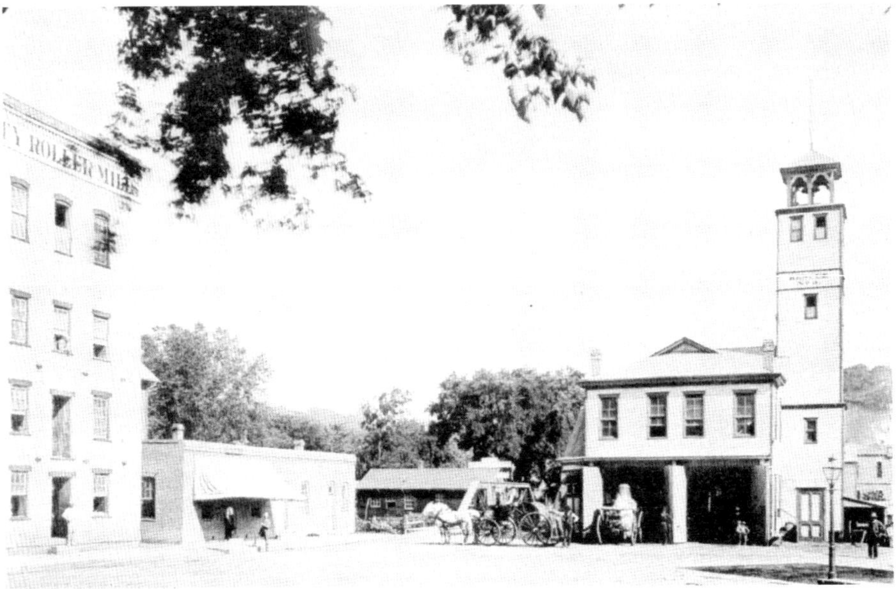

Rescue #3. The first firehouse was a wooden structure with a tall bell tower next to the City Roller Mills and the bridge over Indian Creek. *Courtesy Cal Petersen.*

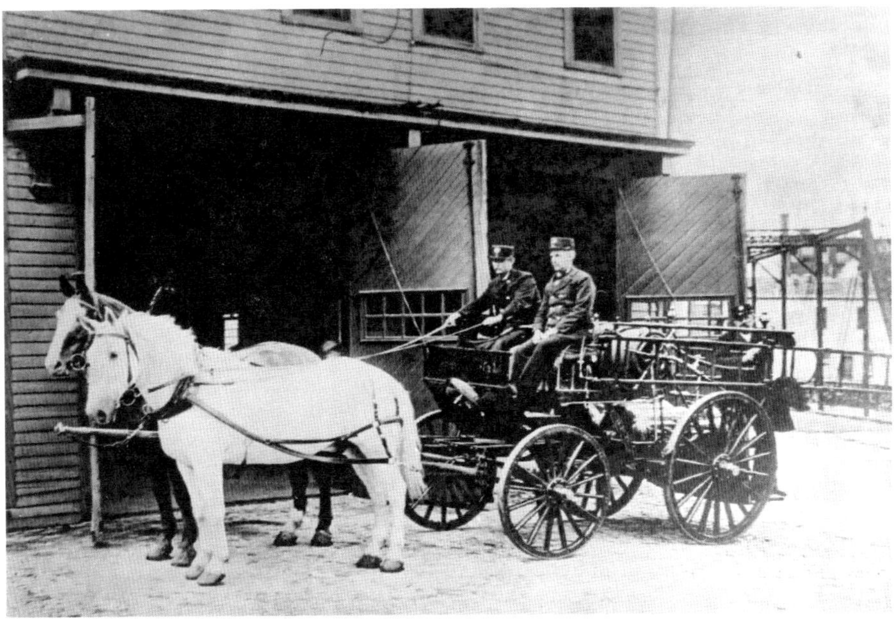

Firemen display their equipment at the barn gates to the original wooden fire station downtown, circa 1895. *Courtesy Cal Petersen.*

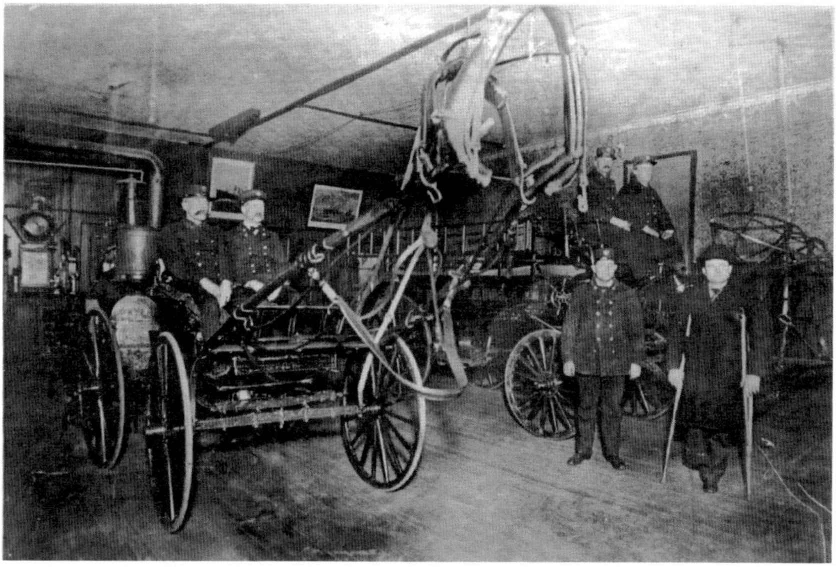

Inside Central Station in 1906, proudly displaying a single horse harness for a steamer. A hook and ladder is in the back. *Courtesy Cal Petersen.*

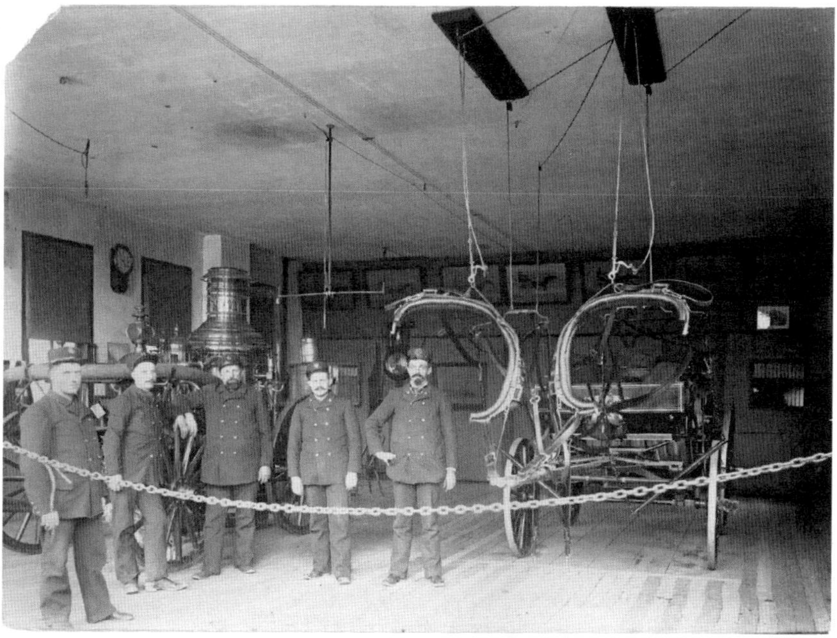

The rigging of the double harness. The horses could be in harness and ready to go within minutes. *Courtesy Cal Petersen.*

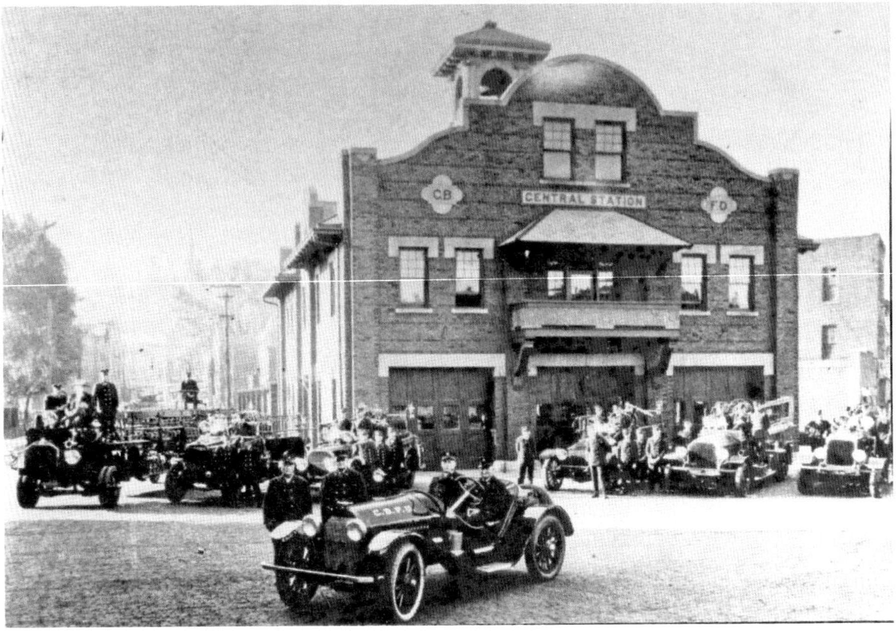

Central Station with vehicles that replaced horses; they were easier to maneuver and didn't need to be unhitched and led away from the fire. *Courtesy Cal Petersen.*

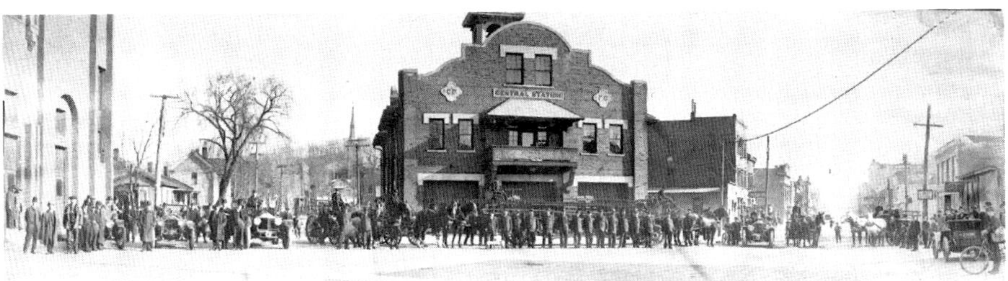

The horse-drawn equipment and motorized equipment and men. The last pair of horses was retired and sold to a local farmer. *Courtesy Cal Petersen.*

On October 9, 1912, the first motorized fire engines were purchased at a cost of $5,500. They were to be used for the #3 firehouse at Bryant and Washington. This was the beginning of replacing the horse-drawn vehicles over the years. The second motorized firefighting vehicle was purchased in 1913. The vehicle was a four-cylinder Webb. As technology changed, motorized vehicles became preferred to horses. The vehicles were easier to maneuver and were faster in arriving at a scene. Slowly, the horses were phased out of service.

V
HOTELS

From the earliest days of the Mormon settlement, the need for lodgings presented itself. Since the Council Bluffs area was one of the gateways via the Mormon Trail to the Great Salt Lake in Utah and, after 1849, a conduit to the gold fields in California, Colorado and Pike's Peak, thousands of people passed through the region. With so many people migrating west, the migrants would need a place to stay as they broke their journeys and resupplied for the long trek west.

Early on, the Mormon settlers in Kanesville first built accommodations for Mormon travelers following Brigham Young to Utah. These early hotels were built of logs, usually two-story dwellings with heavy cloth pasted on interior walls and painted white to give them a less rugged and primitive look. Travelers must have been pretty hard on these hotels, as quite often advertisements in the *Frontier Guardian* boasted of refitting and redecorating the hotels. Because so often the hotels were part of the owner or proprietor's own home, they were referred to as "House."

An 1849 February advertisement in the *Frontier Guardian* for the Union Hotel relates that Mr. H. Clark had fitted up his house in good order for travelers and boarders. By November of that same year, the hotel was under new management and had been completely repaired. An 1853 advertisement for the Union House listed Mr. L. Kline as the proprietor and located the hotel near the courthouse on Hyde Street. Mr. Kline had fitted up his house expressly for the spring migration. He also added that he had a special adjoining building for the sick. There was sufficient stabling to accommodate fifty head of horses and a yard with lots for stock.

Some of the earliest hotels for which we have records included the Bluff House, with proprietor J.K. Cook, located on Main Street (later changed to Broadway). On April 20, 1853, the best hotel stand in Iowa was up for sale. The Bluff House had been improved and enlarged earlier that year and could accommodate a large number of people. The hotel was up for sale because the proprietor was ill.

The Desert Hotel, also located on Main Street/Broadway, may have been sold to a new owner and the name changed, as there is little mention of this hotel. The Robinson House at number 39 Broadway was another two-story log building that later was remodeled with weatherboards. The Robinson House, run by G.L. Robinson, is seen prominently in the early illustrations by George Simons. It was located a little farther west on Broadway from the Ocean Wave saloon. For many years, this hotel was popular and prosperous.

There was also the Kanesville Hotel, which didn't get much mention, and by 1852, the Council Bluffs City Hotel was placing advertisements in the newspaper. The United States Hotel was mentioned only when it became a saloon, the Ocean Wave, or as a locator to the McMahon and William's drugstore. Hotels changed hands often, and names also changed with new ownership, while others retained their original names and reputations. Many people also opened their houses to travelers. An old story tells the tale of a man who welcomed travelers into his home, located a little way out of town and along the trail the migrants traveled. He would take them in for the night, but they never left, and too often he would have a new buggy or horse.

These hotels also served as places for businessmen and professionals to have offices. In the February edition of the *Frontier Guardian*, advertisements announce that Joseph Merritt, attorney, had offices at the Union Hotel, at 226 First Street.

By 1880, Council Bluff City could boast twenty hotels. Business was brisk with all the travelers. Silver had been discovered in Leadville, Colorado, in 1878, creating yet another wave of migrants to keep the hotels busy. Some of these hotels are well remembered and known about for various reasons; some leave tantalizing trails to be researched, and others have left little trace of their existence and are all but forgotten.

Atwood House, located on Lower Broadway, was run by J.W. Dunbar, who announced in an advertisement that the house was kept in a first-class style with a good bill of fare, inviting patrons to drop in and see them.

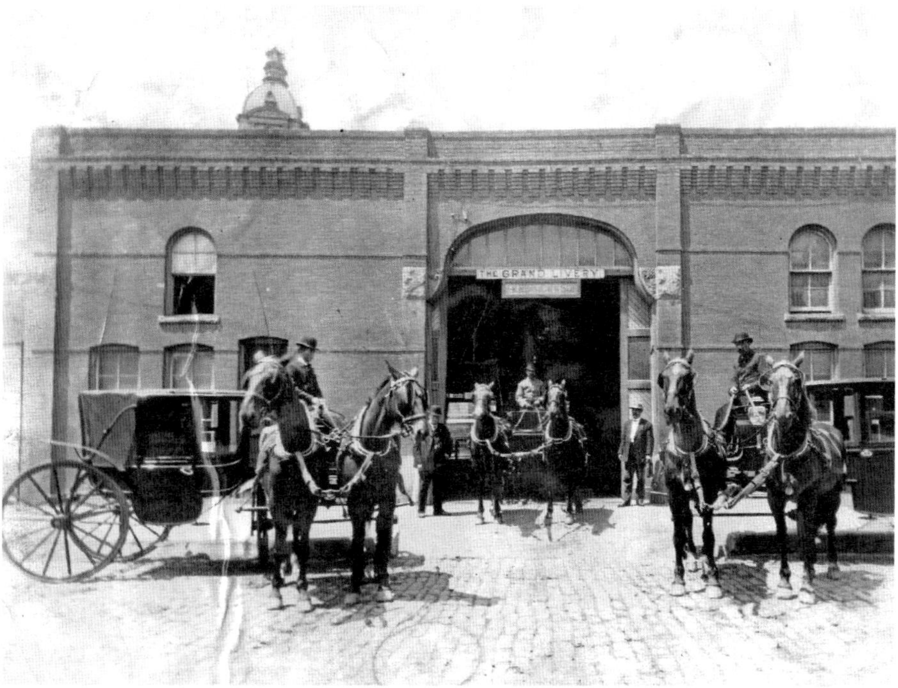

Hinnick & Son's the Grand Livery provided drivers and carriages with teams of horses for rental.

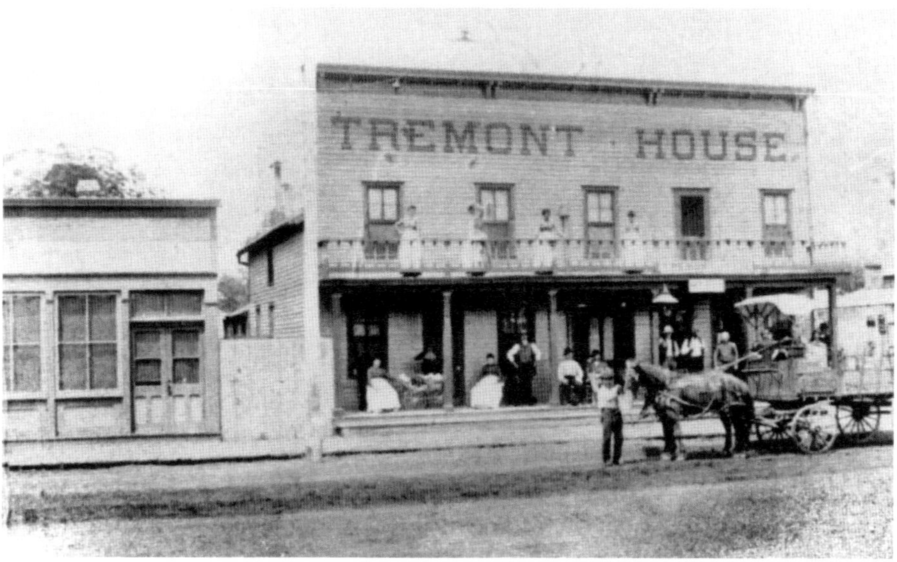

The Tremont on Lower Broadway tolerated no gambling. Across the street in the Wyoming, there could be found such diversions.

There had been more than one Bluff House over the years. The earliest was located at 72 Broadway back in 1853. Before 1897, Peter Basten was proprietor of the fourteen-room hotel located at 1528 Third Street, near Sixteenth Avenue.

Tremont House on West Broadway and Ninth, conveniently located by a number of the railroad depots, was formerly the Metropolitan Hotel, and in April 1871, the old lace underwent the process of cleaning and repainting and was about to start anew under the high-sounding name of the Tremont. J.F. Daniger was the proprietor.

The Farmer's Hotel, located on Middle Broadway, had a successful beginning yet later slipped into shameful notoriety. Early on, the hotel register showed it to be a popular house doing prosperous business. An advertisement on February 6, 1864, relates that the landlord, Mr. Bryant, had opened the building for the coming season. "He is currently excavating in front of the Farmer's Hotel preparatory to putting in a frame addition to his house. His large custom justifies it."

Peter Bechtele had become the proprietor of the Farmer's Hotel by March 28, 1867. Throughout the many histories of the area, his name has more variations of spelling than any other man's in the city.

The Farmer's Hotel is remembered for an incident that occurred in the early hours of 1876. On June 13, William and Patrick Lawn of Mills County had booked a room and were sleeping soundly when a clatter awoke them and rough hands were laid on them. A mob compelled the Lawns to accompany it before the sun crested on the horizon to a location just inside Mills County. Suspected of a crime, the Lawns were given no trial and no chance to vindicate or defend themselves. They were strung up on a sturdy tree branch, and the mob watched them die. They had served in the Union army, and after they were buried in the Catholic cemetery, their comrades placed flowers on their graves on Decoration Day.

The Grand Hotel was built in 1904 in the Lower Broadway area on Bayless Park. For many years, there existed a growing rivalry between Upper and Lower Broadway, with a buffer zone in between. The Grand was built as competition for the elegant Ogden House.

Tragedy struck on the morning of December 3, 1925, at five o'clock, when the sound of an explosion rocked the silence of the darkness. The report sounded like a safe being blown and emanated from the Continental Furniture & Carpet Company. The night engineer had just lit the gas or oil boiler when it blew. He got out as another explosion followed. Fire began to engulf the building. Light glowed on every floor. The fire spread quickly, catching the Shugart Building on fire. The ferocious flames spread across the

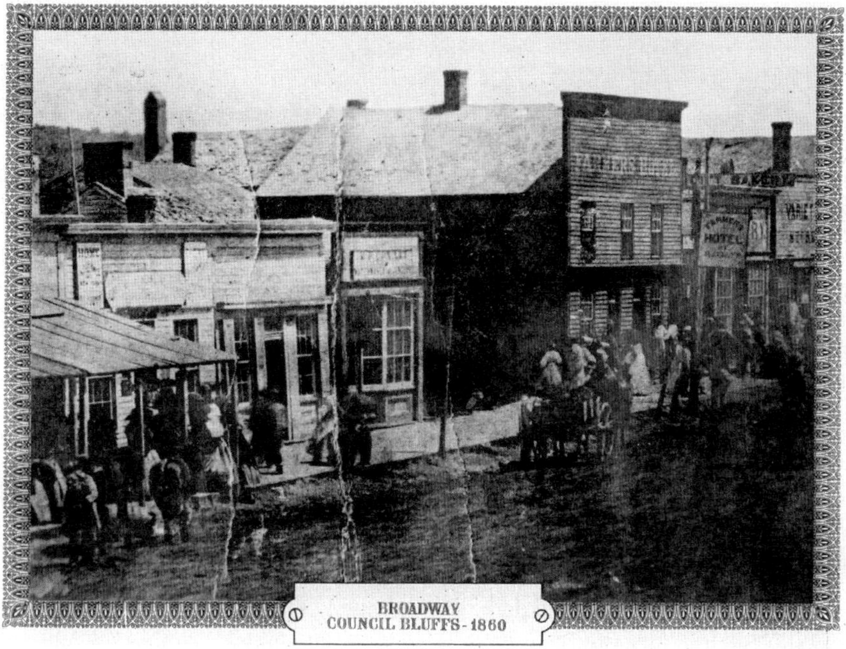

Bechtele's Farmer's Hotel, 1860. The Farmer's Hotel is remembered for the mob that came to lynch William and Patrick Lawn.

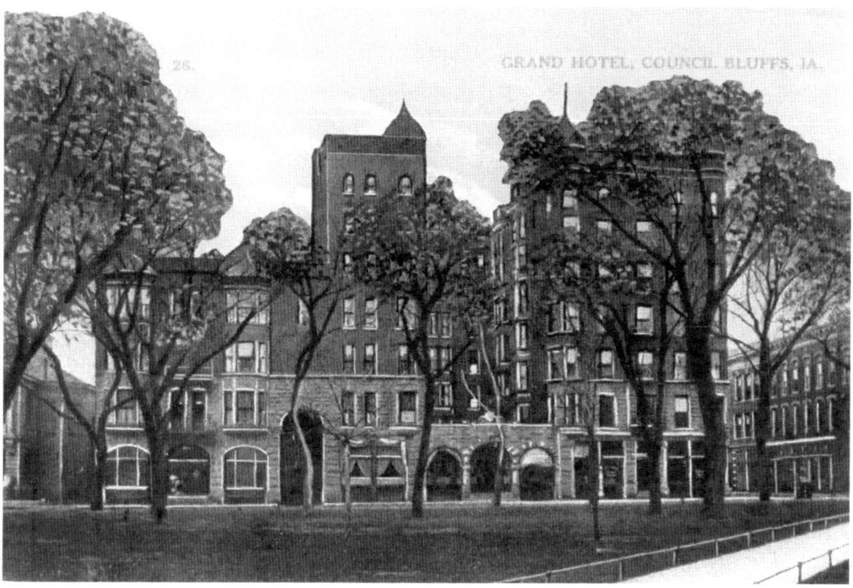

The Grand Hotel on Bayless Park was the finest hotel near Lower Broadway hoping to surpass the Ogden in reputation.

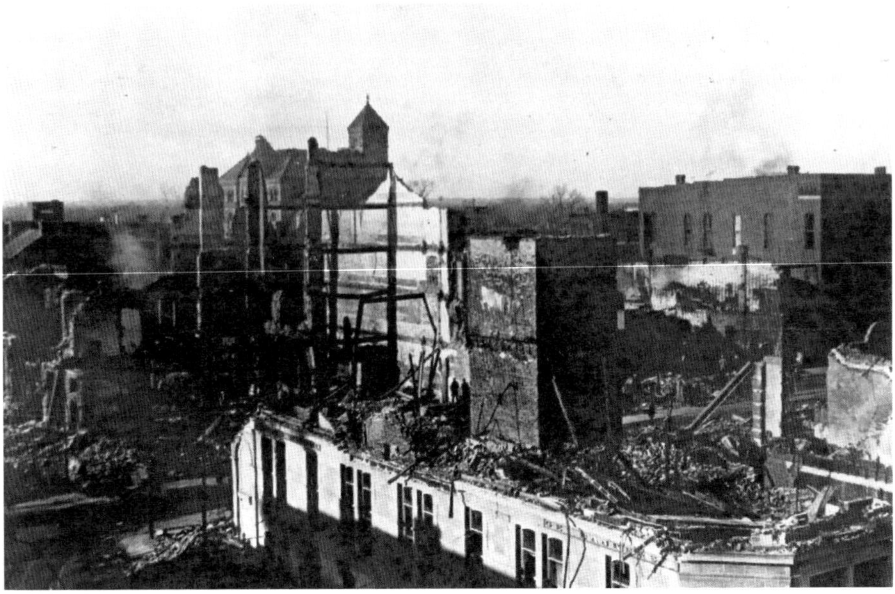

The fire raged through the Continental Furniture and spread across the street as firebrands flew in the high winds, destroying the Grand.

street, and tongues of fire began to lick at the Grand Hotel. Flying firebrands were seen as far as three blocks north and west, reaching Sixth Street and First Avenue. Streets became littered in ash and charred wood.

The fire destroyed the Citizens Gas and Electric Company building. The Shugart Building, five stories in height; the Smith Building; New York Publishing; and two stores, all with basements, were burned to the ground. All seven stories of the Grand Hotel were laid to waste. Only shells of these buildings remained.

Of special loss in this fire were the efforts of Mrs. Mattie Harl, a resident of the Grand Hotel. She had been working for years on compiling an extensive history of Council Bluffs. She had been interviewing early residents for quite some time; those pioneers were long dead, and those memories were tragically lost in the fire.

The Chieftain Hotel was built in 1927 with 153 rooms. It replaced the Grand. The murals in the Corn Room and Pioneer Room were painted by local Iowa artist Grant Wood. When they remodeled, the owners no longer saw any value in the original murals. They planned to paint over them. A man who was wise enough to recognize their unique worth carefully removed them. Over the years, Grant Wood's work has become iconic of his era, and a few of these murals have returned to Council Bluffs and are on display at Iowa Western Community College and the Pottawattamie County Courthouse.

The Chieftain Hotel ceased to be a hotel, as travelers no longer chose to stay in the downtown area. The old hotel was refurbished in 1970 and renamed Bluff Towers, repurposed as housing for senior citizens and persons with disabilities.

Hotel Goodrich was located at the corner of Eighth Street and Broadway. Walt Goodrich had been an employee of the Northwestern Railroad for sixteen years and then worked in other hotels in the city before building his own complete hotel with a café and its own bar.

Fire plagued the hotel on March 8, 1922, when flames gutted the stairway and elevator shaft and damaged part of the first floor. Every room in the hotel suffered some damage. The intense heat destroyed furniture, walls and fittings on the entire ground floor, except for the kitchen and dining room. The damage was most severe by the elevator shaft, which acted like a chimney, drawing the fire upward. The day porter, Roy Talbot, discovered the fire when he came on duty at 5:45 a.m. for his shift. He acted quickly, woke the night clerk and alerted patrons. Each room had a rope ladder to

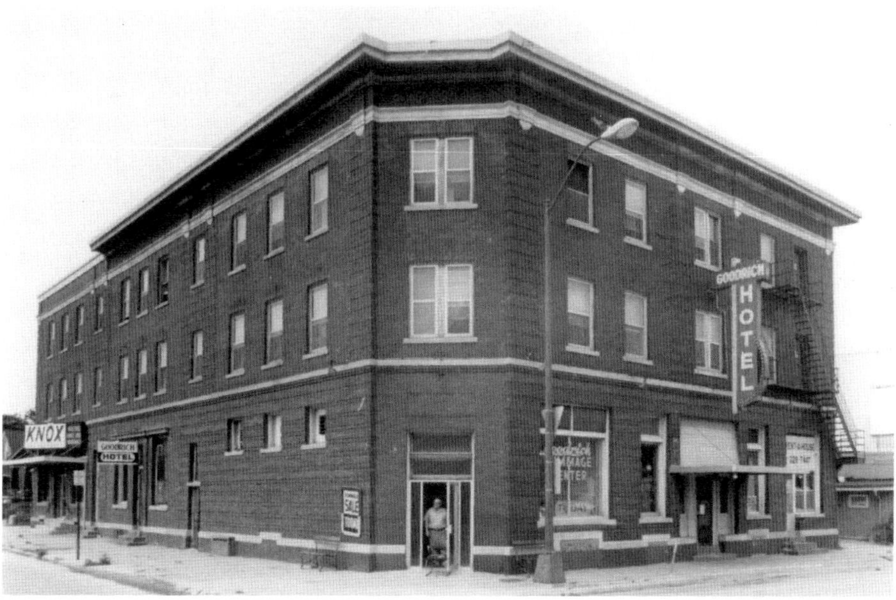

Hotel Goodrich, at 801 West Broadway and built by Walt Goodrich, opened in 1906. The Goodrich survived until 1984, marking the end of an era when it was torn down.

toss out the window for the patrons to escape. Firefighters were able to get the blaze under control quickly.

In later years, as the commercial traveler no longer supported the older hotels, the Goodrich became a residence hotel for men. No ladies were allowed beyond the first floor. The Goodrich was fondly remembered as the place where the churches held rummage sales. The Hotel Goodrich survived longer than any of the other downtown hotels. When it was torn down in 1984, the end of an era passed with it. Where the Goodrich once stood is yet another parking lot.

Merchant's Hotel on Lower Broadway placed an advertisement in the *Nonpareil* on September 12, 1868, announcing that this house was completely new and fitted up in first-class style, having all the modern improvements with regard to comfort and convenience of travelers. Reed and Imeson were the proprietors

In an 1874 advertisement, the Metropolitan Hotel boasted of its central location in the city, near the principal railroad depots, and that the street railway passed directly in front of it. The advertisement announced that the hotel was thoroughly furnished, and for business and commercial travelers, it offered the very best inducements. The rate was two dollars a day. Ed Snow was listed as proprietor. On August 23, 1862, the Honorable John A. Kasson was stumping for his candidacy for Congress, and an excellent farewell supper was given at the hotel for him.

Two fine hotels were built near the courthouse. The Creston House, built by Mr. Mohn, began as a small hotel, but as patronage increased, so did the hotel. Also, the Keil at 501–07 Main was one of a number of hotels built opposite the courthouse as that area grew in 1877. Originally a two-story hotel, a third story was soon added to accommodate the wealth of travelers who passed through the city.

Gerspacher's Union Avenue Hotel (not the same as the Union House mentioned earlier) had previously been the Chicago House, located on Broadway, but the proprietor renamed it because the new street, Union Avenue, would start nearby. As of December 7, 1878, the signs had already been changed.

Unfortunately, the hotel wasn't able to retain a good reputation. Over the years, a disreputable clientele took roost there, and unsavory events cast a dark shadow over the hotel. Canada Bill Jones and his gang of bunco men made use of the hotel in the 1870s. When Canada Bill was not riding the rails in search of someone to ensnare in a game of three card monte, he would look for willing victims at train stations and in the hotel, men who wanted to take a chance on winning while he fleeced them thoroughly.

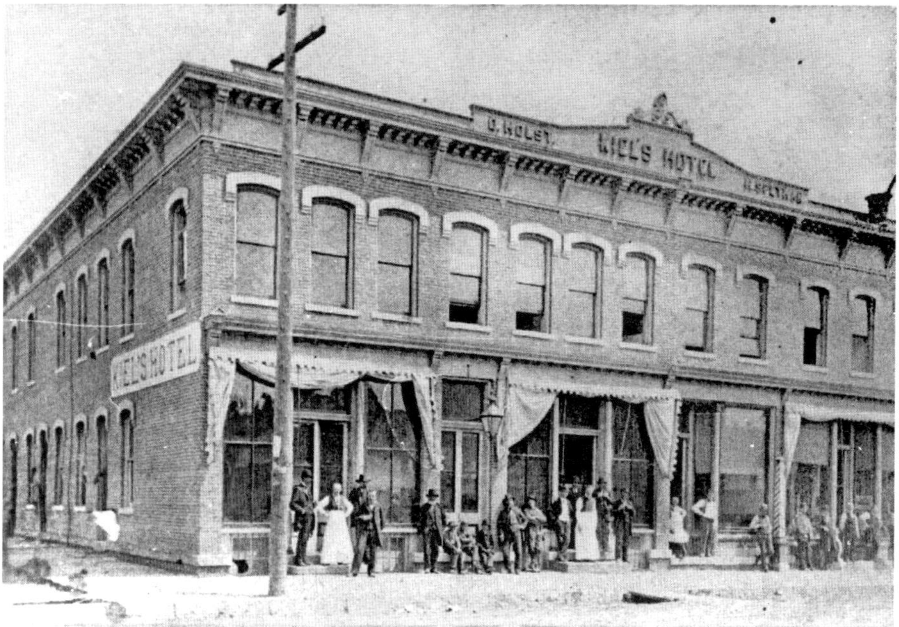

The Keil at 501–07 Main was one of a number of hotels built opposite the courthouse as that area grew in 1877.

In 1883, a wall was built in front of the Union Avenue Hotel to meet the height of the newly established grade in the city. Even the streetcar tracks along Broadway were raised. But that couldn't restore the hotel's good name.

Other unsavory characters who tarnished the reputation of the hotel were Matt Curran and Three Finger Jack Roach. Gerspacher himself had a run-in with the law. He was charged with assault with intent to commit murder by a resident of the hotel.

Major Williams, a notorious confidence operator, shot and seriously wounded his partner, James Hughes, at the Union Avenue Hotel on December 17, 1885. Williams fled but was caught by Monday night. Evidently, a fight broke out between the two men over $2,000, the take from a recent con. Williams, up to the time of his impending death, refused to talk. One of the rounds fired shot off the proprietor's finger, but he later claimed he hurt it in a doorjamb.

A number of hotels whose names have turned up here and there in research have little information to tell us more. The Waverly Hotel was listed as one of five hotels in the area in 1856. The Lion's Den, as it was once called, was a small hotel dating back to the 1870s, across from the old

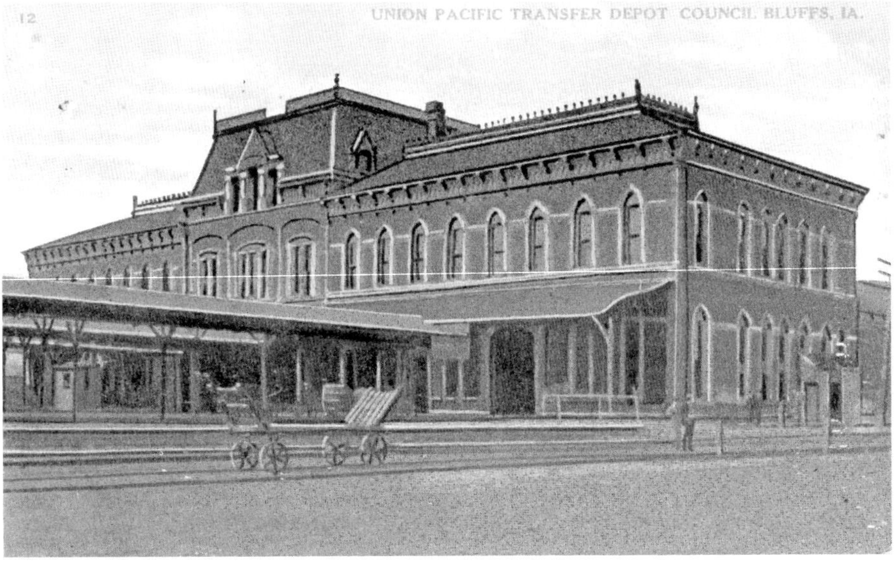

Union Pacific Transfer Depot and Hotel was built at the transfer depot to save travelers the trouble of staying downtown overnight before catching their next train.

YMCA. It was converted to apartments and removed about 1990. And there was Platner's House—again we have a mystery with a name associated with Ira Platner, the Ocean Wave and the United States Hotel.

The Lion's Den was listed as being located one block west of Bayless, on the edge of Victorian Row. It was a small hotel that was converted into apartments and was finally razed just into the new millennium to make way for another car park.

Union Pacific Transfer Depot and Hotel was a three-story brick hotel constructed at the transfer depot to save travelers the trouble of staying downtown overnight before catching their next train. By 1938, a more modern building was demanded, and the hotel was remodeled. The hotel was gone by December 4, 1953. It is now a park with a giant golden spike to commemorate the joining of the railroads at Promontory Point, Utah. Mail arrived by train.

By 1856, there were five hotels listed in the area: Union House, the Robinson House, the City Hotel, the Waverly and one of the finest of them at this time: Pacific House.

Pacific House

One of the most iconic hotels in the history of the city was the Pacific House, the first of the great hotels built by Mr. Samuel S. Bayless. He arrived in town as one of the thousands heading west for gold but chose to stay. He saw needs and supplied them; his industriousness helped change and build a modern city.

Migration had ceased by July 1852, as the wagon trains wouldn't leave any later in the season for fear of being caught by winter storms. The town, once the majority of Mormons migrated, was reduced drastically to a population of about five hundred. An outbreak of cholera claimed the lives of many who remained. In the spring of 1853, the influx of travelers picked up once again, swelling the population.

The extraordinary influx of strangers during the spring and summer of 1853 prompted Bayless to build what he hoped would be the finest hotel in town. He had recently platted the land he'd purchased from departing Mormon Henry Miller; it became the First Bayless Addition and included much of the downtown area of Broadway, Main and Pearl Streets.

It was Samuel Bayless who is responsible for the interesting angle on Broadway that occurs at the intersection at Fourth Street. He built his hotel at that turning place so as to call greater attention to it.

For his hotel, Bayless erected a three-story building with attics at 518 West Broadway and Scott Street. He built it in brick, and so it would catch the eye of the visitor, he painted it yellow. A gracious, wide veranda fronted across the façade of the hotel's first two stories. Pacific House was completed just before Christmas 1853. For the grand opening on Christmas night 1853, Mr. Bayless gave a ball, and the revelry of this gala event went on until dawn. It was declared the finest hotel west of Des Moines and north of St. Joseph, Missouri.

This new hotel towered over other smaller wooden, log or weatherboard buildings that surrounded it. The Pacific House was not the first building constructed in brick; this year, many new buildings were erected using that material, as so many fires had taken their toll on the older weatherboard and log structures. Though brick was more durable, it did not guarantee that the structures would not catch fire.

When the Nebraska territories were opened in 1854, Secretary Thomas B. Cuming and territorial governor Francis Burt arrived in Omaha. Burt was ill but took the oath of office anyway and was sworn in as governor on October 16, 1854. Two days later, he died, thus promoting Thomas Cuming to territorial governor. It was two months before Cuming's twenty-sixth

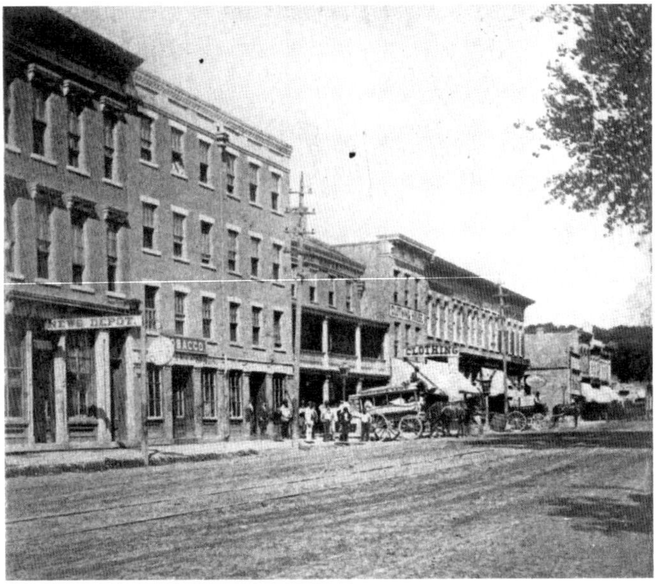

Pacific House with its bricks painted yellow and its gracious, wide porches. At one time, it towered over its wood-frame neighbors.

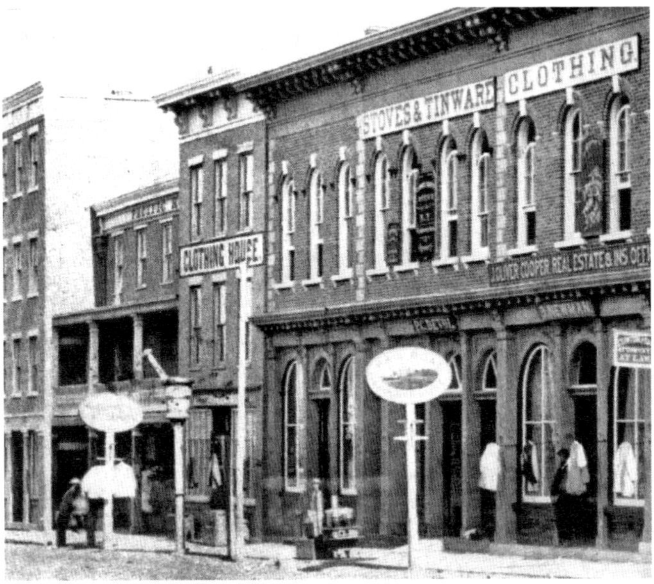

Pacific House, once the tallest building on the block, is now sandwiched between newer buildings that dwarf it.

birthday. Evidently, he and his wife, Marguerite, were not too impressed with the primitive lifestyle and rough accommodations of the new town of Omaha in Nebraska Territory and opted to take up residence in Samuel Bayless's well-appointed Pacific House, located in Council Bluffs. From his hotel room, Cuming conducted the business of running the territory. Thus, the Pacific House served as the seat of government for territorial Nebraska. Nebraska became the thirty-seventh state in 1867.

Another visitor of note arrived in Council Bluff City and lodged at the Pacific House. In August 1859, a tall, slender railroad lawyer stopped in Council Bluffs for a rest before heading on to his next city as he stumped for his candidacy for president of the United States. His name was Abraham Lincoln. He stayed at the Pacific House along with Judge Test of Indiana and Illinois secretary of state Ozias Hatch.

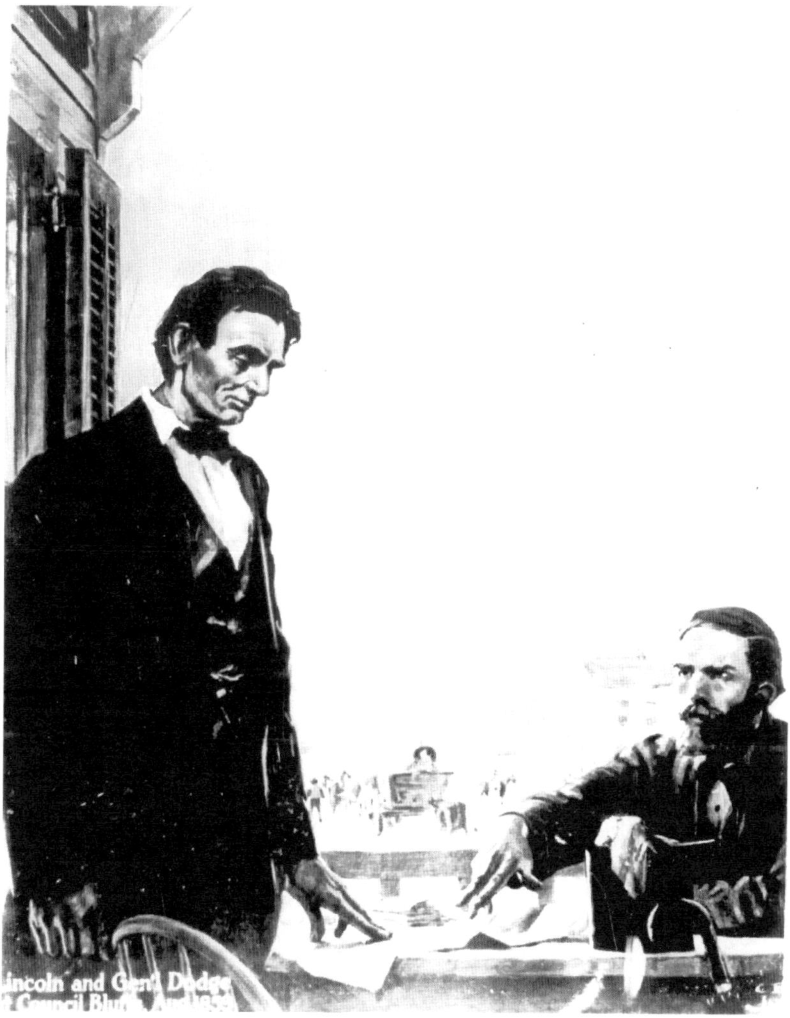

Lincoln and Dodge on the veranda of the Pacific House discussing the possibilities of the railroad.

They had come to town by steamboat. As he closed his campaign tour, he was invited to rest before heading back east. Lincoln and his party were delayed in their departure when the engine in the steamboat broke down. News spread quickly about his visit. People heard he had come to town and came to petition him to speak to them. Lincoln kindly obliged and spoke to crowds from the wide balcony of the Pacific House in the early evening. So many more wanted to hear him, so he was persuaded to address the people at a concert hall in town.

A public reception was given in the public reception rooms of the Pacific House. Hundreds of people attended. Lincoln also had time to visit with his friends William Pusey and Thomas Officer, who hosted another reception for the presidential hopeful. Nearly every citizen in town came to meet the man from Illinois and shake his hand. A fortuitous meeting happened between Lincoln and Grenville Dodge, who joined Lincoln on the veranda and spoke to him about the most excellent path for railroad travel. He suggested it pass through Council Bluffs on its way west. Later, Lincoln awarded Council Bluffs the honor and distinction of being the eastern terminus on the way west for the railroad. Though there was no bridge, the building of the line began in Omaha until a proper bridge could be constructed.

Another notable visitor arrived at the Pacific House a few weeks later: Lincoln's rival Stephen A. Douglass. He, too, spoke to the people who came

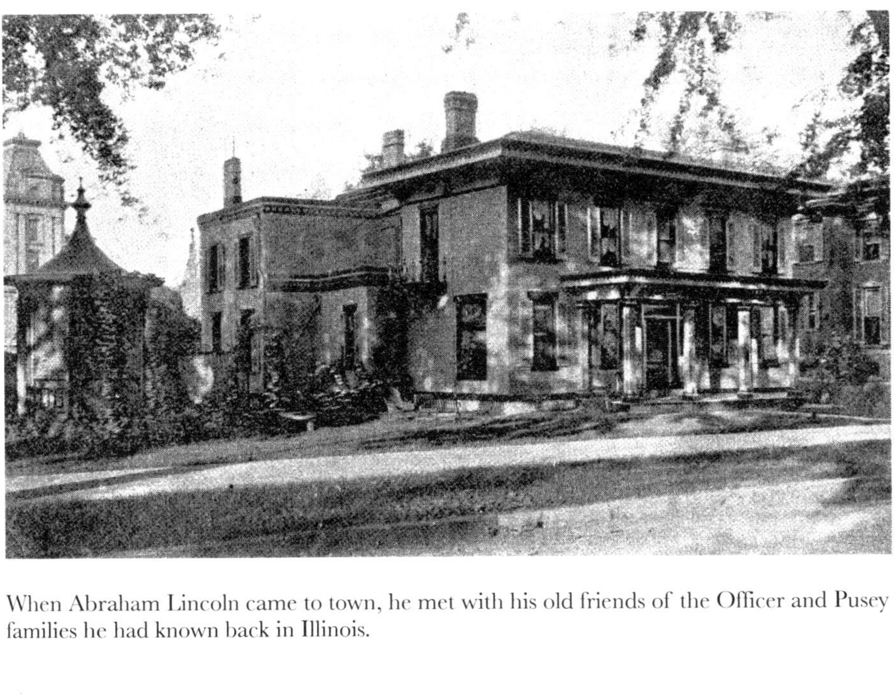

When Abraham Lincoln came to town, he met with his old friends of the Officer and Pusey families he had known back in Illinois.

to hear him. After the Civil War, Generals Sheridan and Sherman stayed at the Pacific House. They, too, spoke from the balcony to the people. Not everyone was notable, but some made the papers. For example, a beautiful young woman was discovered dead in her room at the Pacific House from an overdose of morphine after being disowned by her family.

People flocked to the Pacific House. Soon, there was more demand than rooms. In 1863, Bayless added a southeast wing to the hotel. Still, demand for rooms was high. Ever improving the Pacific House to keep up with demand, by March 30, 1869, Dr. Bragg, the manager, had enlarged and refitted the hotel, adding an L-shaped addition on the northwest side of the building. He also enlarged rooms, with each room now having two windows. The halls were also widened, perhaps as a way to compete with the newly built Ogden House. Additionally, Bragg built a new four-story brick addition. It was the first four-story building on Broadway. For many years, Pacific House remained the principal hotel in town. The hotel measured 140 feet on Broadway and 204 on Scott.

On the cold and frosty evening of January 11, 1872, the Pacific House caught fire. It began in the northwest wing. To make things worse, winds kicked up and pushed the fire into the main part of the building. A defective flue in the rear of the north wing, where the kitchens were located, was blamed for starting the fire. The fire burned for a while before being detected. Around 2:00 a.m., a man returning from an Odd Fellows function in Omaha saw the fire and sounded the alarm, rousing sleepers.

Frightened people saved what they could of their trunks and possessions. Others saved some of the hotel furniture, piling it in the street. One well-meaning but confused man tossed a mirror to the pavement below. He then proceeded to carry the husk mattress out of the burning building. The streets were crowded with people watching the fire or helping remove contents. People had turned out to witness the fire and do what they could to help. They also loaded wagons with goods from businesses nearby in case the fire spread.

There was no official fire department yet. The city had to rely on the many volunteer fire departments. The volunteers did what they could to save the building. Problems occurred as the cistern ran dry. Because Indian Creek and the bucket brigades were not sufficient to fight fires, the city had placed a good number of cisterns strategically about the area. However, during this fire, the cisterns ran dry, and firefighters had to go to the creek for water. They frantically cut holes in the ice, drawing buckets of water to throw on the fire. It wasn't enough. At about 3:00 a.m., the front wall fell out into the street.

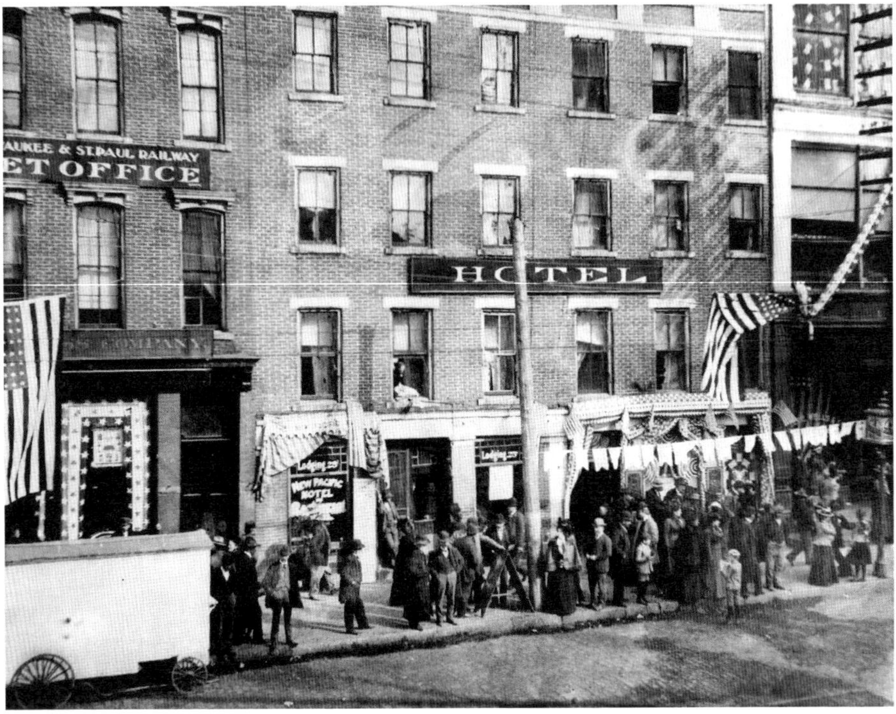

The Pacific House was enlarged as it was rebuilt after a fire. The façade was flush with the other buildings, and the gracious double verandas were gone.

Firemen managed to save as much of the original structure as they could. Extensive repairs were made, and the Pacific House was back in service by 1873, now with three hundred rooms to serve clientele.

The New Pacific House boasted many amenities for its patrons. In 1872, a beautiful new bar was installed. Ed Rogers' saloon, with the refitting, became the most spacious bar outside St. Louis. There was also a barbershop run by Fritz Bernhardi, a Prussian emigrant; a number of offices for professional men; and of course, an abundance of rooms.

In January 1889, a story about the refitting and remodeling of the New Pacific House let patrons know that the floors were removed and replaced, and the windows had been refitted in keeping with the quality the hotel offered to its patrons.

The wide, gracious porch was gone with the rebuilding, and by now other buildings on each side had been erected in brick. The Pacific House was dwarfed by its new neighbors. In 1898, advertisements for the New Pacific House said it had forty-five rooms available that could be rented for $1.50

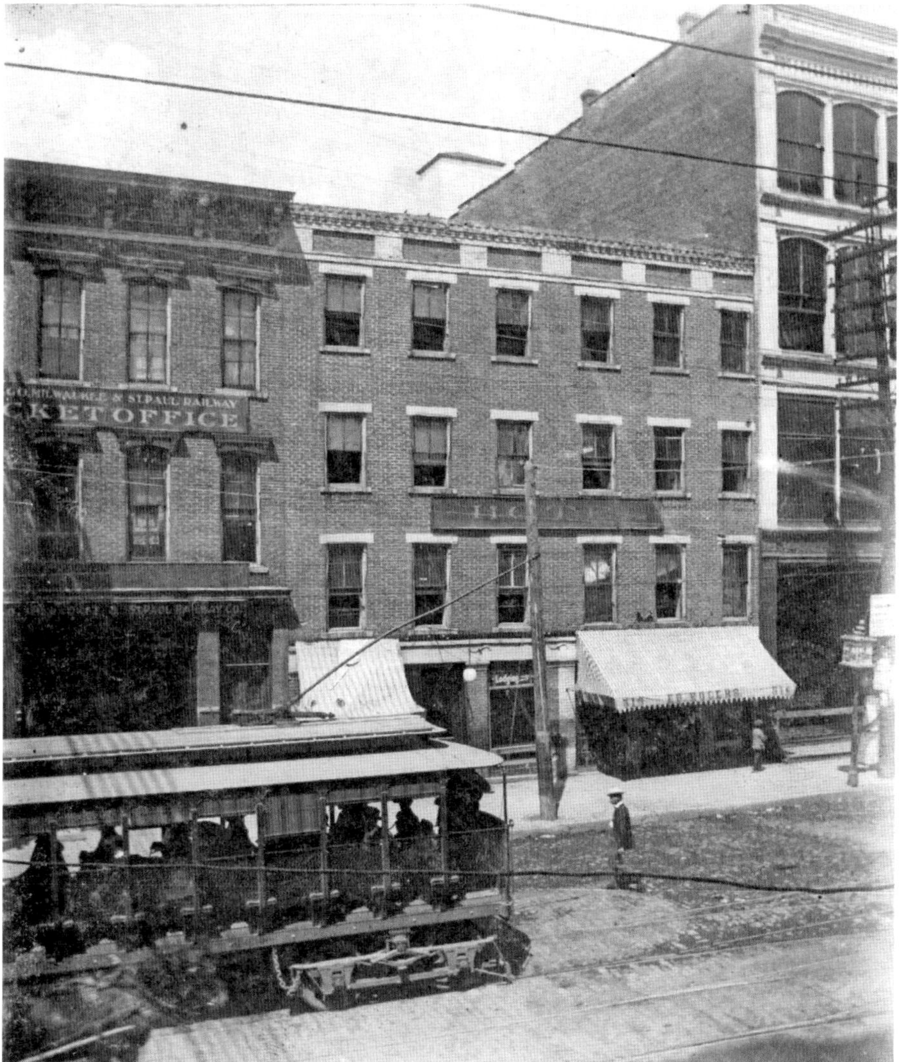

Streetcars pass in front of the Pacific House. Council Bluffs was the second city in the nation to have an electrified transport system.

or $2.00 a day. In 1898, the major hotels listed in a souvenir book were the Ogden, Grand, Kiel, Neumayer, Creston House and the Pacific House, under its new name the Inman.

The building of the Ogden House in 1869 presented the first rival to the Pacific House in popularity and elegance. Other hotels were built in the city, and they dwarfed the Pacific House, now seemingly wedged between much larger brick structures. Times were changing; the Eisman Building had been erected next door.

By 1889, the Pacific House name had been changed to the Inman Hotel. The glory days of the Pacific House were in the past. Patrons were demanding things the hotel could no longer provide, and the hotel was razed in 1893. The five-story Wickham Building at 522 West Broadway replaced the old hotel. On March 11, 1917, the Wickham block itself was heavily damaged by fire.

The Pacific House had not been the only hotel in Council Bluffs City over the years, but it was one of the pioneers, providing the best to its guests. Other hotels have had their share of clientele and even some scandal or notoriety attached to their histories.

The Neumayer

Jacob Neumayer, born in Germany, came to America in 1867. He worked in a number of hotels before he bought the Bryant House in 1882 for $5,000. He remodeled it and put his name on the hotel. By 1888, he had found this hotel to be too small for the demand of customers wishing accommodations. He built a beautiful three-story structure with a full basement. Later, he expanded again with a brick and stone addition, giving the Neumayer a frontage of seventy-two feet at 208 West Broadway with a depth of 150 feet into the alley. It faced the corner and park.

In May 1897, the old part of the hotel burned. Jacob Neumayer rebuilt on the site of the old hotel, placing the frontage uniformly along Broadway, with iron and plate glass windows in front. The hotel had its own gas generator and seventy-five rooms, all fitted out with all the latest amenities of lighting, giving patrons both gas and electric lights. The building was heated by steam and decorated with modern furnishings. It offered travelers sixty-six rooms, a large dining room, a barbershop, a bar and a pool hall.

Room rental ranged from $1.00 to $1.50 per day. For the convenience of the hotel's patrons, streetcars passed in front often. The Neumayer even had a fine brick barn for housing travelers' coaches and teams. This large stabling barn was located on North Second and Vine, with fifty stalls and a large lot to the west, with sheds for wagons and surreys. For added security, a caretaker lived in small quarters on the premises. Once the automobile

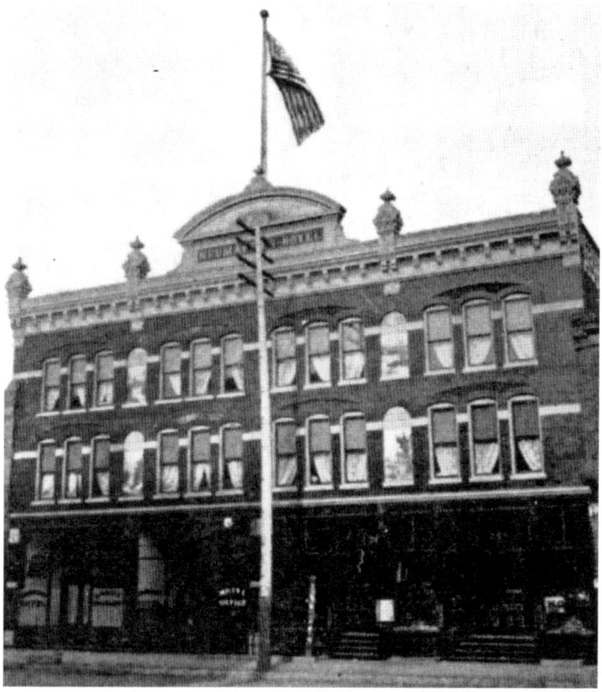

Right: Jacob Neumayer opened his hotel in 1882 and later expanded it, adding many more comforts and amenities.

Below: The Neumayer's saloon was on par with the amenities offered in other hotels. Alcoholic beverages could be enjoyed amid potted palms. Atop the pillars were eagle sculpture and spittoons.

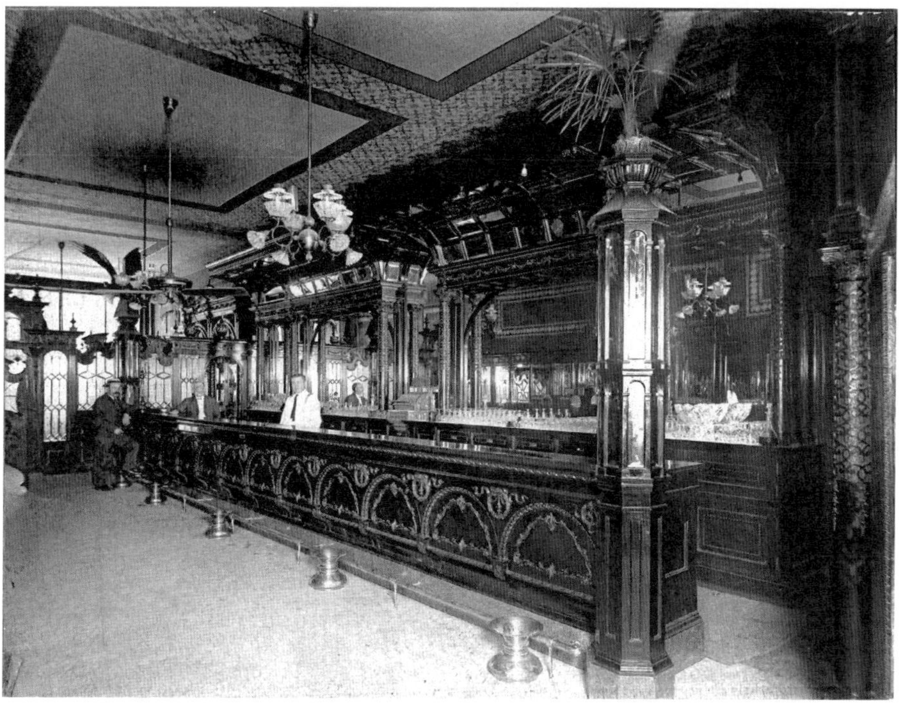

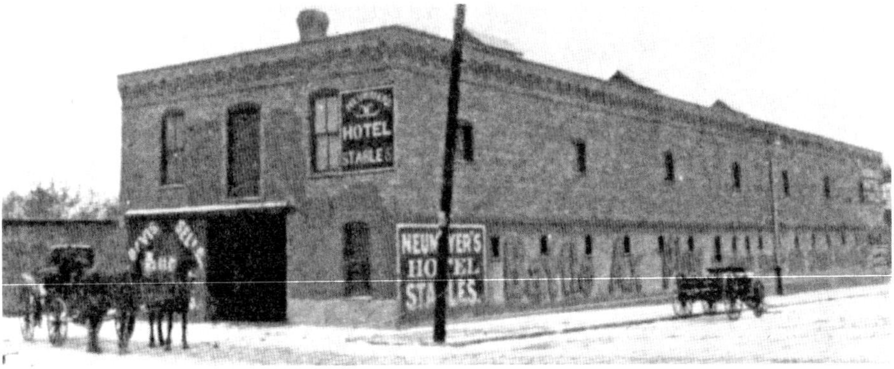

The Neumayer provided an excellent livery for its patrons. A caretaker lived on the premises. Once the livery wasn't needed anymore, the building was used for storage and finally torn down.

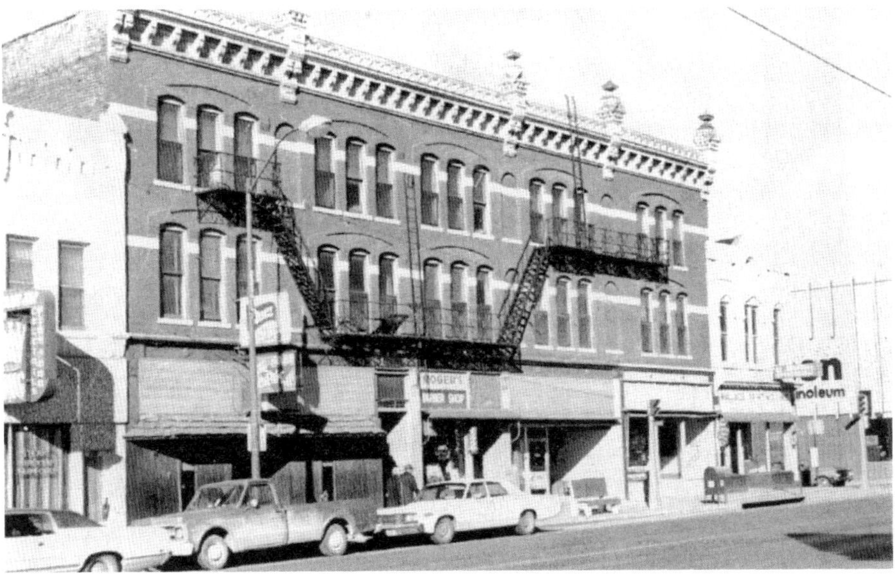

The Neumayer was sold and renamed the Bluffs Hotel shortly before it was razed along with so much of the downtown area.

replaced the use of horses, the Neumayer rented out the livery to businesses for storage. The stables, built in 1882, lasted until 1952, when they were torn down. Lucas Neumayer followed his father as hotelier.

When Neumayer was killed in an accident in 1932, the hotel was sold to the Knox family, who also changed the name to the Bluffs Hotel. Old glory faded into the mists of memory as the hotel went the way of other aging hotels in the city. In 1959, the cornice and ornate trim were removed in an attempt to modernize the building before its demise.

Ogden House

As more and more railroads came to Council Bluffs as a hub, the need for more hotel rooms became apparent. A group of businessmen saw the need for adequate hotel facilities and began to plan for the building of an elegant hotel to meet the needs of travelers. In February 1869, these prominent citizens met in the storeroom of Mr. J.H. Warner and discussed the building of this hotel on Broadway, just east of the Methodist Episcopal church. They raised $10,000 in donations, which proved to them that the citizens were in favor of building this new brick hotel that would be a showplace. The site was purchased, and in the spring they began to build a three-story structure with an additional mansard story.

The owners decided on the name as a tribute to William B. Ogden, former mayor of Chicago, for his energy that contributed to developing this section of the country through the completion of the Northwestern Railway. Thus, they called their new hotel the Ogden House.

Heavy rains fell that summer, delaying the laying of the cornerstone until May 12, which they celebrated as a gala day. It coincided with the arrival of the first train on the Rock Island Railway. People stood in the pouring rain undaunted. At the Ogden House, Mayor Bloomer, as master of ceremonies, lowered the immense cornerstone into place after depositing some coins and relics in the cornerstone. That evening, banquets were held utilizing three venues, as so many people attended, followed by a ball held at the Pacific House, which the elite of the city attended along with the railway officials and visitors.

The event of the winter season of 1869 in Council Bluffs City was the eagerly anticipated opening of the new Ogden House at 171 West Broadway. The building had been completed and was regarded as the handsomest, most complete hotel between San Francisco and Chicago. The owners furnished it in the most elegant manner.

On December 22, 1869, the doors were thrown open to the most brilliant assemblies that ever met under any roof on either side of the Missouri River. Guests were present from far and wide. A lavish banquet was given in honor of the opening, which five hundred guests attended, and there were twenty-one dances, including the quadrille and highland fling.

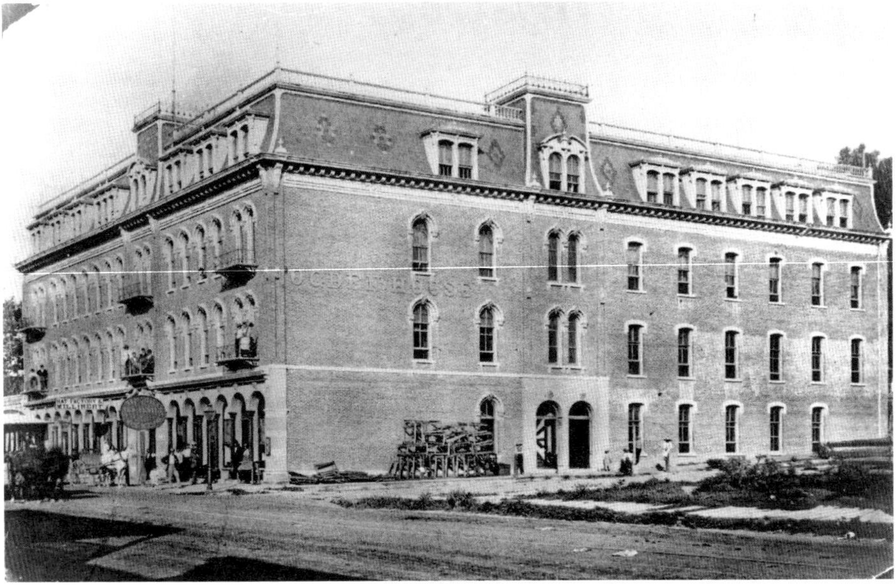

The Ogden House opened for business on December 22, 1869. It was the finest hotel between Chicago and San Francisco.

On October 21, 1874, at just after two o'clock in the morning, a *Nonpareil* reporter sat at his typewriter pounding out a breaking story as the sky glowed a gaudy orange, sending unstable light flickering across the ceiling. The architectural pride of the city, the Ogden House, was being devoured by fire. Flames were discovered in the upper northeast corner, and the first alarm rang out over the stillness of the night.

Soon after, church bells rang, alerting citizens, who dressed and hurried to the scene to see if they could assist in any way. They stood about in dismay, to find the Ogden House enveloped in flames beyond the control of the fire department.

The fire began on the third floor in room 61 or 62 as a result of a bursting lamp. William Garner, one of the proprietors, and clerks tried to douse the flames with pails of water. The flames caught on the bedding and filled the air with a blinding, suffocating smoke, and they were forced to abandon their efforts. Flames spread up into the mansard roof area and broke through the roof, casting a lurid light on the darkness. The building burned slowly from the top down, allowing the staff and guests to save the furniture from all but the upper floor.

The fire department did what they could using the steamer and pouring two streams of water onto the flames. After the fire burned out, the walls remained standing for a few months until a gale finally toppled them.

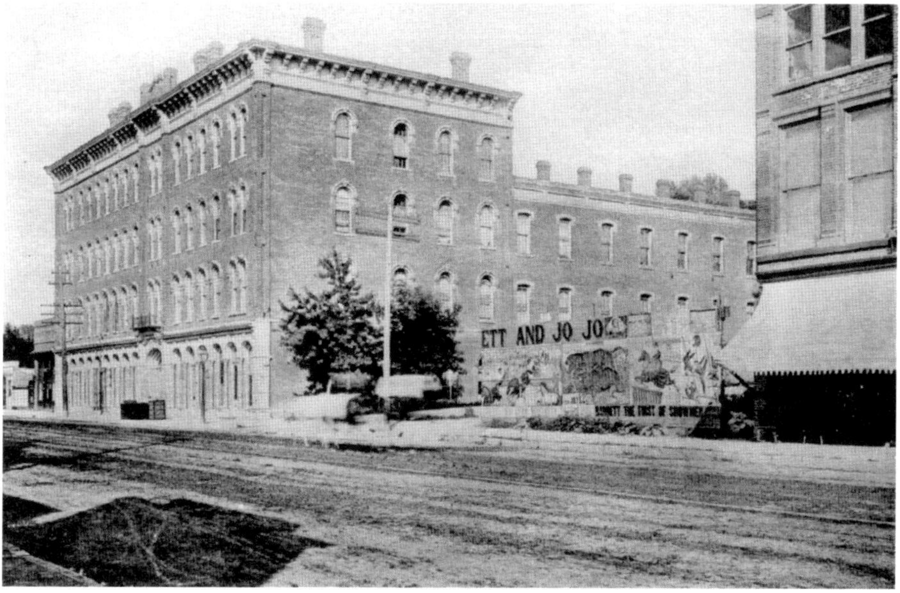

The New Ogden House rebuilt, taking its place as the finest hotel once again.

Undaunted, the owners decided to rebuild the Ogden even better than before, but this time avoided the French-style mansard roof, as it had kept the fire department from getting to the exposed part of the building in time to save it.

The appointments within the hotel were some of the finest: beautiful black walnut woodwork, carpets from Brussels and a grand dining room with the capacity for five hundred people. Huge mirrors imported from France hung on the walls, and there was a black-and-white marble checkerboard floor.

The hotel had fifteen-foot ceilings, and the hall on the floors with the guest rooms was fourteen feet wide and fourteen feet tall. The first floor of the hotel included the reception area, with a hand-carved walnut reception desk and walnut stairs and banister. There was also an elegant bar, a billiard room, a full laundry and spacious kitchens. The second floor had offices, a dancing hall, a parlor for ladies and a separate parlor for the gentlemen, along with a smoking room and a reading room. There was a Spinet grand piano on the second floor—one of the first pianos built by Steinway. Floors three and four were dedicated to the sleeping rooms and suites. Bedrooms were elegantly furnished with black walnut three-piece bedroom suites consisting of a bed, a commode and a dresser. There was a large sink built into the wall upstairs.

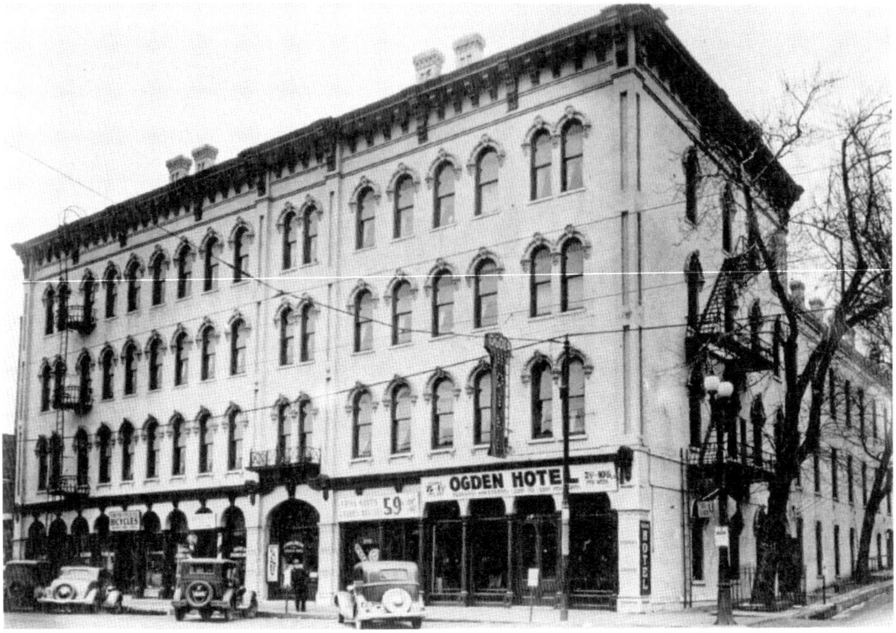

The glory of the Ogden House had begun to fade in the 1920s as the needs and travel habits of patrons changed.

The New Ogden once again became one of the largest and finest hotels in the area, where the best class of commercial travelers would stay. Advertisements would boast that the Ogden House was located in the city center, with 150 finely furnished rooms. It has four iron balconies in front and stores on the ground level. Over the years, improvements continued in order to keep the Ogden as the finest house for its patrons. In 1888, elevators were added, along with all modern improvements. The hotel was illuminated by electric lights utilizing its own private power plant.

By the 1930s, the glory days of the Ogden House had passed. The Ogden was no longer considered the finest hotel and began a downhill slide that would end in its destruction. In 1937, the Ogden went bankrupt. The automobile replaced the train as the way to travel, and the downtown location for a hotel wasn't as desirable as it had been. The Ogden became a resident hotel for a number of people.

The owners tried to revitalize the old hotel. In November 1975, plans were made to have the Hotel Annex added in 1911, remodeled into thirty or forty luxury apartments. This plan never came to realization. In February 1977, the Ogden lost its license, and all residents moved out, evicted. The

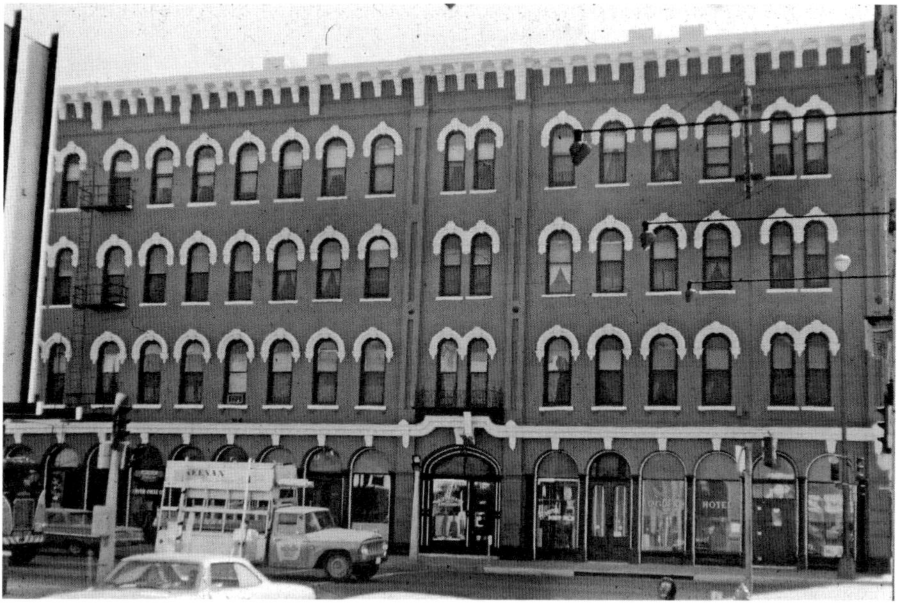

The Ogden House hosted members of Alcoholics Anonymous, who sat in worn metal chairs at Formica tables under the reflection of elegant French mirrors.

Ogden would never reopen. One of the residents, "Blackie" Robert Black, had lived there for twenty-five years. He took pleasure in living in the room where Grant stayed decades before.

The handful of residents packed their meager possessions and were relocated. The building was boarded, awaiting what would come next. Owners placed the old hotel on the National Register of Historic Places and waited. Unfortunately, vandals assaulted the building. The fine marble flooring in the dining room was torn up. The elegantly hand-carved walnut banisters were marred, spindles were destroyed and newels went missing. The light fixtures were ripped out. A group of people toured the building, hoping to save the landmark, on August 19, 1981. What they found shattered their hopes. They found the building in a desperately sad state of disrepair. The wallpaper was stained and peeling away from the walls, paint was cracked and peeling away from surfaces, the roof leaked badly and the destruction wrought by the vandals had left the fireplaces and wood moldings torn up and bathroom fixtures destroyed.

Many of the old furnishings were still in the rooms. A set was saved and is on display in the Union Pacific Museum. Other pieces were auctioned off.

The once magnificent Ogden House, the pride of the city, was torn down in 1982. As the building was razed, the original cornerstone was uncovered.

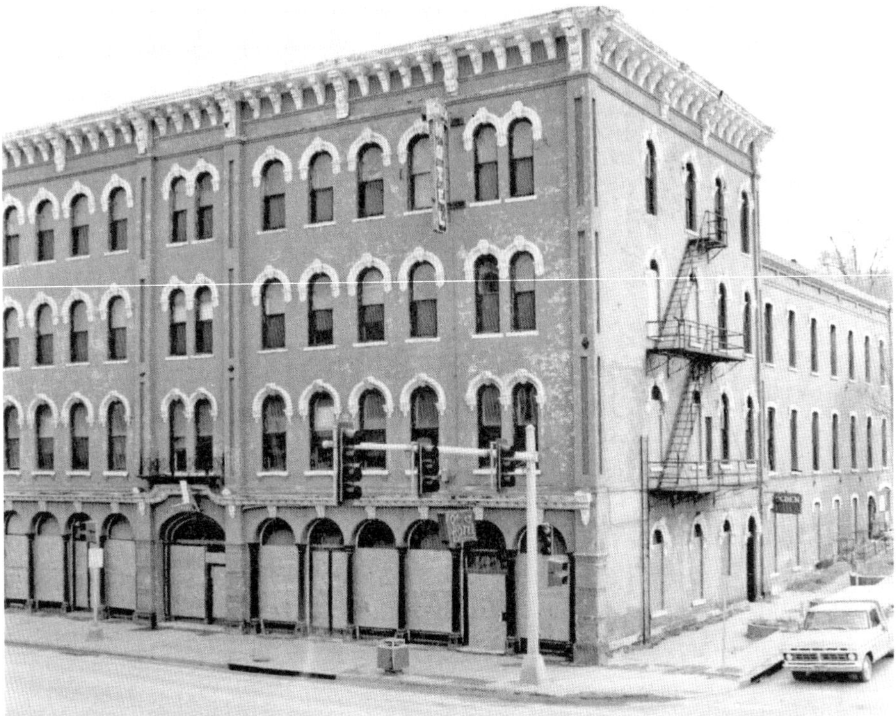

The Ogden House vandalized—they destroyed what they could. The building was razed in 1982 to make way for a car park.

The cornerstone had long been hidden since the time the city raised the level of Broadway by some four feet. Inside the cornerstone was found a metal box with thirteen coins and other memorabilia that Mayor Bloomer had placed there in 1869.

The debris was cleared away and the land paved for a parking lot—a sad ending to what was once the finest hotel between Chicago and San Francisco.

Travelers still passed in and out of Council Bluffs. The railroad wasn't the hub of activity as it once had been. Passenger trains dwindled as people drove in cars instead. More modern hotels were built, like the Comet Motel three miles past the south Omaha Bridge on Highway 175; the Motor Inn; and in the 1960s, the Chalet Motor Lodge, erected at 1530 Avenue G. The latter had all the amenities that modern travelers desired: a swimming pool, banquet room, air conditioning, TV and nightly entertainment.

Just as the hotels of the previous century have gone the way of the wrecking ball due to changing times, so, too, have these motels failed to stand the test of time.

VI

ENTERTAINMENT

Entertainment had always been a great part of the life of the city. From the time the Mormons dwelt in the area, halls for entertainment, dances and assemblies were constructed. These halls were first built of logs, then weatherboard frame buildings and, finally, brick. The first dramatic performance was staged by amateurs of the Forrest Dramatic Association in 1856. When the old concert hall burned down—possibly the old Hyde's Hall that is lost in the mists of time—Mr. Beebee took it upon himself to provide the city with a new hall. December 25, 1857, marked the opening of a new concert hall. Beebee Hall opened on Christmas Eve with a dedication, a lecture, a concert and a dance. The gala opening was attended by 160 couples of the city's elite and fashionable set. Unfortunately, the new hall was in ashes by December 30, 1857.

Another popular assembly hall was Burhop's Hall, which sat on the north side of Upper Broadway. Some productions had a little more excitement than others. In the winter of 1868, Joseph Mueller, a music teacher, produced an operetta with twenty young girls. There were some special effects planned for the performance.

Just as the chorus of young ladies stepped onto the stage, taking their places and forming a semicircle, an enormous report that sounded like a cannon going off rattled through the hall. *Boom!* The audience, of course, jumped up, gripped by fear, as an offensive odor of gas rushed into the auditorium. Some of the stagehands rushed into the girl's dressing room, which they had exited a moment before the explosion was heard. They discovered that the special effect red light for a later scene that a druggist had carefully prepared had exploded when the chemicals came in contact with the air. Fortunately, no one was hurt; however, the explosion tore out two windows and burst the panels of two doors, shattering them. Burhop's Hall had been renamed Platner's Hall by the late 1870s.

The concert hall where Lincoln addressed the crowds was built in 1854 by J.M. Palmer on the northwest corner of Broadway and Sixth Street. At about 3:00 a.m. on February 22, 1860, the hall was discovered to be in flames. It was surmised that the fire had started after a performance given the previous evening. The hall was being used for a school function; sawdust had been spread over the floor, and possibly a spark had fallen into the sawdust and smoldered before taking hold.

Mr. Babbitt also built Babbitt's Hall, for dramatic productions and assemblies, in the Phoenix Block. The Phoenix Block was located on the south side of Broadway. Mr. Babbitt had a stage built at one end of the hall, and many leading citizens took part in the amateur dramatic productions. Some of these included *The Forest Rose* and *Paddy Miller's Boy*. George Simons painted the scenery and drop rolls for the theater. The U.S. land offices were also in the building. The Phoenix Block was destroyed by fire.

Sol Bloom built Bloom's Opera House, which spanned the block from Pearl to Main. Bloom was a wholesale grocer. He used the Stewart and Haas Building to store groceries and other heavy goods. On November 9, 1867, the central supports in the cellar of the building gave way under the weight. The entire building collapsed. A few people were buried in the rubble but survived. An article in the *Nonpareil* in 1880 gave a detailed account of the renovations taking place in Bloom and Nixon's Hall. Because of the demand for its use, these renovations were pushed through quickly and the hall reopened.

On August 2, 1864, Mabie's circus set up its tent and had a show in progress when a fearful windstorm kicked up across the area after dark. A great blast of wind collapsed the pavilion, extinguishing the lights. Several thousand patrons were plunged into total darkness under the fallen canvas. To add to the confusion, one of the lions escaped for a short time before being captured. The canvas of the pavilion was torn to shreds as the frightened patrons trapped under it ripped their way out. No lives were lost, and no one suffered severe injuries.

Another story relating to the circus that began in about 1859 also has a connection to one of the first churches in town. J.S. Haskell had a little over a nine-month tenure as pastor of the Congregational Church. He had been a showman and was described as having been a fakir and performer adept at the sleight of hand, as well as being a ventriloquist. He left none of his stage theatrics out of his exhortations in the pulpit. His sermons became dramatic displays of a solo act. He was a man with a fondness for horses, and he owned a large number of teams and managed a freighting business to supplement the meager pay of the pulpit. Others described him as being quite sensational and possessing loud manners on the street when driving his horses. Others claimed he had a weakness for alcohol.

Either way, his tenure at the church ended abruptly. He disappeared quite completely. No one saw or heard from him again until his return in 1870 as the manager of a circus. As he drove one of the circus wagons through the streets of town, he was recognized. He wasn't a man one would easily forget. Those who remembered him hailed him cheerfully; they even gave him a standing ovation, reveling in the humor of his transformation. When addressing the crowds, he alluded with lighthearted humor to his previous employment in the city. He even demonstrated the semblance of piety that had thinly veiled his true character: that of a natural and irrevocable buffoon.

Dohany Opera House

John Dohany spent many successful years in the livery business. But it wasn't enough. He wanted to give back to the city by providing a special place for the culture he enjoyed so much. With this in mind, he built his livery stables with a special use for the second story: an opera house.

The original Dohany Opera House, built in 1868, was located on the second floor of the livery stable on Bryant Street. It made parking convenient for a patron's horse-drawn carriage. However, the fragrance of the stables tended to waft upward into the house, causing more than one lady to hold a perfumed handkerchief to her nose during a performance.

Despite the fragrance of the stables below, the Dohany Opera House attracted some of the best performers of the day. Many names that would have meant something to the citizens of Council Bluffs City in the 1800s mean little to the audiences of today; their names have faded into obscurity. However, there are some performers' names that were displayed on the boards of the Opera House that are still recognized even today.

On April 19, 1877, William F. "Buffalo Bill" Cody appeared at the Dohany Opera House, playing himself in *The Red Right Hand—or Buffalo*

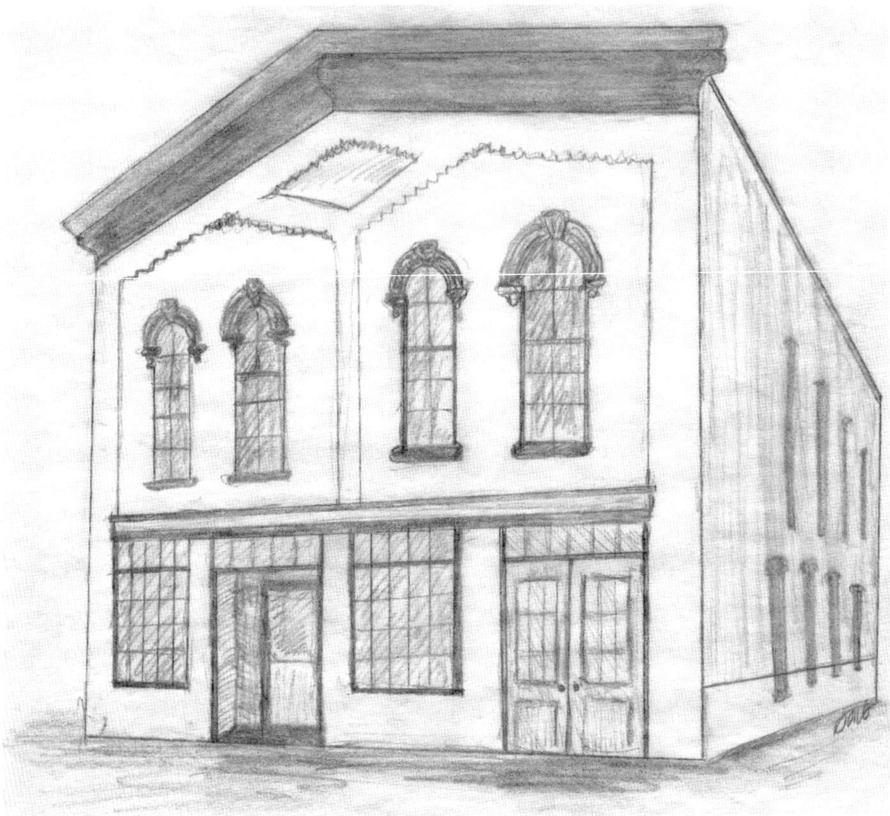

The 1868 Dohany Opera House, built over his livery stable. The fragrance from the horses made its presence known, coloring each performance.

Bill's First Scalp for Custer. Though politically incorrect in today's world, it was touted as a new western drama and was well attended everywhere it played.

Some of the well-respected theatrical performers who graced the stage in 1878 included Maggie Mitchell, Kate Claxton, John T. Raymond, Lawrence Barrett, Henry Ward Beecher and Robert Ingersoll.

Maggie Mitchell was born in 1832 in New York. She began her acting career at age twelve, appearing in many walk-on parts for children. Her role as the heroine in *Fanchon, the Cricket*, adapted from a George Sand story, created quite a sensation and became her signature role throughout her entire career.

Kate Claxton, born in New Jersey in 1848, first played mostly comedy roles. When she played the role of Louise in *The Two Orphans*, she became regarded as one of the finest emotional actresses of her day.

John T. Raymond, born in Buffalo, New York, made his theatrical debut in 1853, and his career evolved via low-comedy parts. He played Asa Trenchard in *Our American Cousin*, but his signature role was as Colonel Mulberry Sellers in Mark's Twain's *Gilded Age*, adapted for the stage.

Lawrence Barrett was born in 1838 and raised in Detroit, Michigan. He was a Shakespearian actor and frequently worked with Edwin Booth. It was said that he could show depth of sorrow with the merest movement of a muscle.

Robert Ingersoll was born in New York in 1833. He was a lawyer, political leader and orator and served in the Civil War. His nickname was "the Great Agnostic." He gave lectures around the country, speaking about free thought, humanism, abolitionism and women's rights. His friend Walt Whitman said about him, "It should not be surprising that I am drawn to Ingersoll, for he is *Leaves of Grass*."

Henry Ward Beecher, a Congregationalist and Presbyterian clergyman and social reformer, toured, speaking against the Free Love movement and advocating for temperance and women's suffrage. He supported Social Darwinism, embracing Darwin's theory of evolution. He was an unusual speaker for his era in that he employed humor and informal language, including dialects and slang. His sister, Harriet Beecher Stowe, was an abolitionist and writer. She wrote *Uncle Tom's Cabin*.

In direct contrast to Beecher, the controversial Victoria Woodhull also was featured, though at a different program. She was a leader in women's suffrage, an activist for women's rights, a labor reformer and an advocate for Free Love. This movement wished to grant women the rights to marry, divorce and bear children without government interference. Many of her reforms have been implemented over the years. Others are still being debated today. She was also the first woman to run for president of the United States as a member of the Equal Rights Party. Shortly before the election, she was arrested on obscenity charges for publishing an alleged affair between Henry Ward Beecher and Elizabeth Tilton. This added sensation to the coverage of her candidacy; however, she received no electoral votes. Beecher did finally admit to the affair and was tried.

Though most of the performers were from out of town, on May 2, 1872, Dohany's Opera House welcomed back a young woman who had grown up in Council Bluffs. Early on, she had displayed quite a wonderful musical talent. It was in town where she had her start in theater. The famous prima donna Miss Fanny Kellogg performed to a hometown audience that packed the house to overflowing. She returned again in the summer and fall of 1882. She was always well received.

Other performers of worldwide fame who graced the Dohany Opera House stage included Ole Bull, born in 1810, a Norwegian violinist and composer who toured several times through America. He spent time in Paris with many of the great musicians. Franz Liszt heard Ole Bull play his own compositions and admired his work. Bull's music has a simplicity and a longing but is not easily played. Bull heard Paganini play and wanted to write music that would not be easily mastered. He bought land in 1852 in Pennsylvania and established New Norway, a colony for his fellow countrymen. He discovered a young man, Edward Grieg, and toured the United States, Europe and Cuba. He associated with the musical community in Paris in the 1830s, creating beautiful music that echoed Norwegian folk music. Franz Liszt praised Ole Bull, stating that Bull was "a savage genius who moved me."

John William Boone, known professionally as Blind Boone, was a black pianist who toured the country after the Civil War. He was born a slave, and the name of Boone came from his ancestry, tracing back to servants of Daniel Boone. Mrs. George Sampson of Iowa learned of the talented black child and gave Boone lessons in the classics on the piano. He had an amazing ear for music, and after hearing a tune once, he could play it. He is well known for bringing ragtime and other black music to the concert stage. He had a custom-made nine-foot oak grand Chickering piano that he toured with. This piano is in a museum in Columbia, Missouri, where he lived.

Robert Browning, the poet married to Elizabeth Barrett Browning, would do readings of his poetry. "My Last Duchess" in particular lent itself well to performance.

John W. Drew, a well-known temperance speaker, came to Council Bluffs more than once, filling the hall with his impassioned call for prohibition. If the temperance movement had succeeded, half the businesses in town would have been shuttered. Bars and saloons were one of the larger business interests in the city. An election was held on June 27, 1882, regarding prohibition. Citizens gathered on the streets to express their opinions of the push for prohibition. Women were in support of prohibition and stood on one side of the street, while the beer and liquor men stood opposite. Bands employed by the liquor men played music from wagons. Signs and slogans expressed their views: "Down Fanaticism, Give Me Liberty"; "Let every man decide what he pleases"; and "Vote for Prohibition. Vote to protect your homes and your families. Vote for God and your Country." The majority of city dwellers were against prohibition while the rural voice favored it. A heated contest ensued.

The opera house gave many years of service to the community; however, in 1894 the theater was declared unsafe and was closed. The livery stables

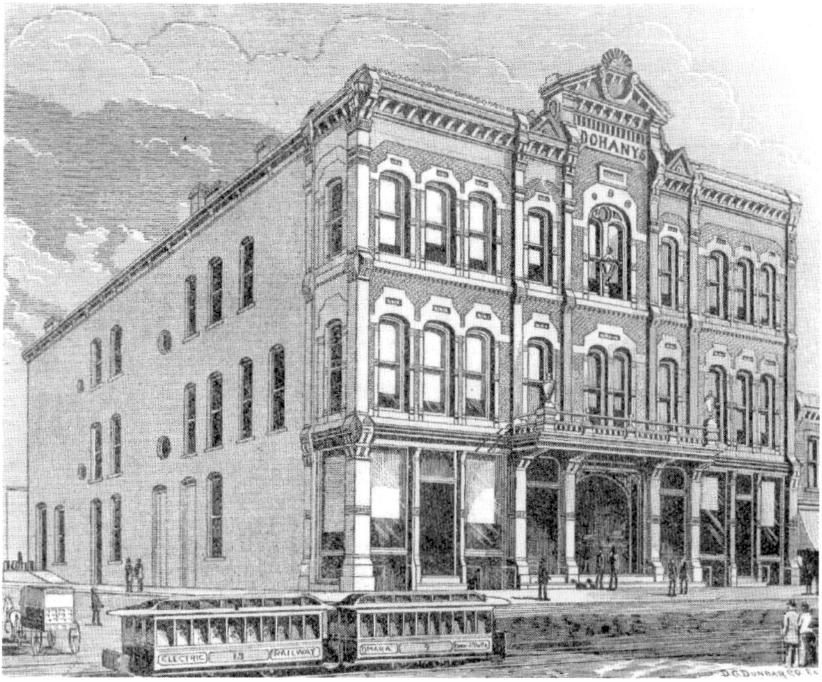

The New Dohany Opera House at Sixth and Broadway was built with every modern convenience, with none of the fragrance of the previous opera house.

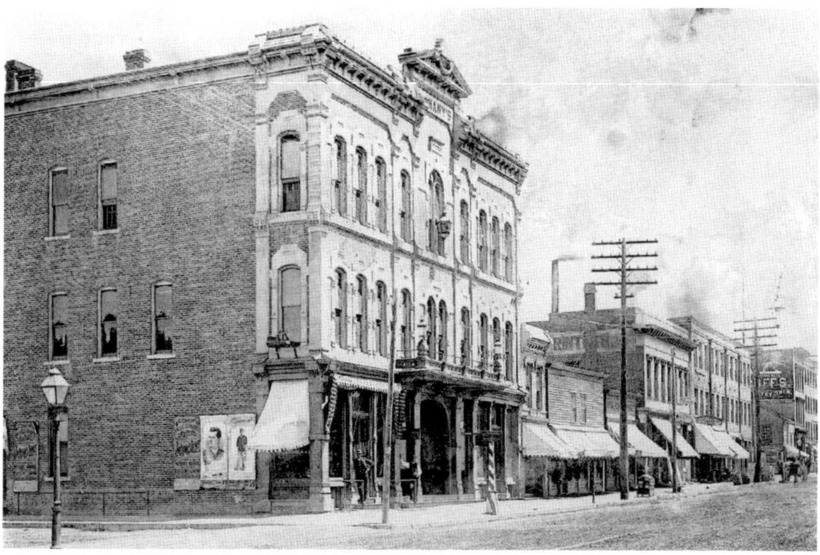

The New Dohany Opera House was a grand success. Performances played to a house that could hold 1,400 patrons.

continued to be used, and the upper floor, though shuttered, became a place of storage for other merchants. Sometime in the late 1920s, the building was torn down. Before its destruction, the *Nonpareil* ran a story that stirred memories of those who attended performances in the old opera house. A photo taken from the balcony shows piles of goods stored on the floor and the stage empty and silent.

When the old opera house was deemed unsafe, Dohany built the New Dohany Opera House in 1894 on the corner of Sixth Street and Broadway at a cost of $65,000 to $75,000. This new theater could hold a house of 1,400 patrons. He fitted it out with all the latest improvements and conveniences. Every ten minutes, a streetcar would pass in front, making it a very convenient location.

In 1916, the New Dohany theater changed hands. Owned now by A.H. Theaters, the name was changed to The Strand, shedding its connection with

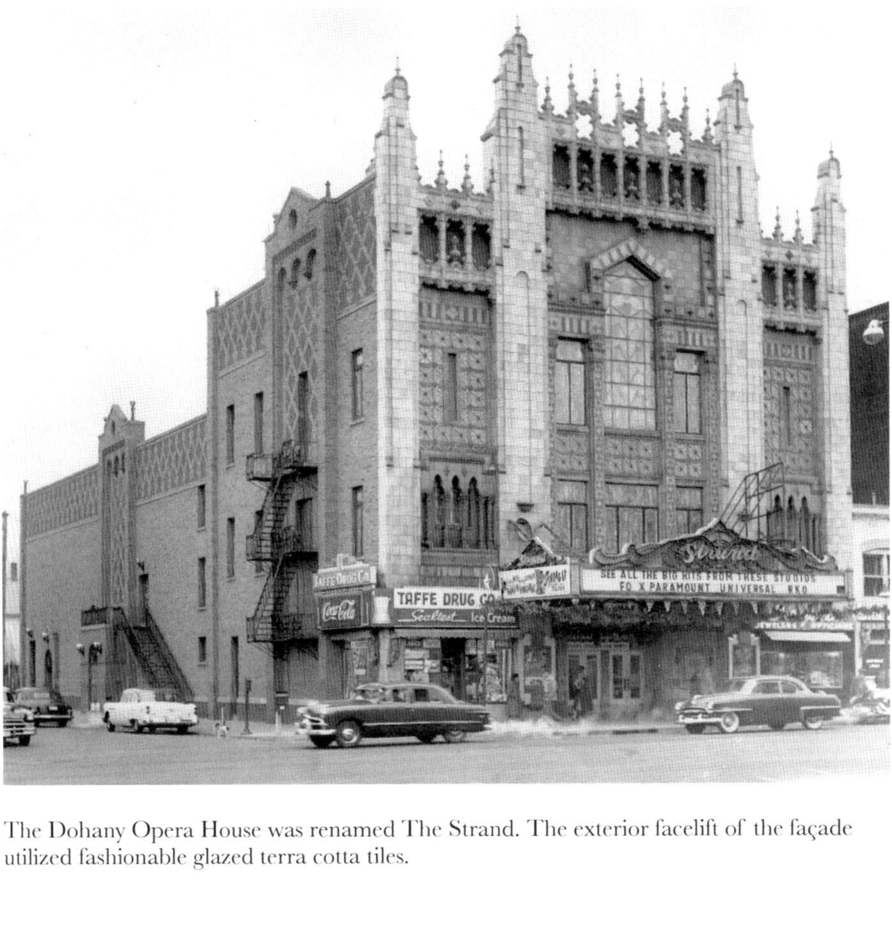

The Dohany Opera House was renamed The Strand. The exterior facelift of the façade utilized fashionable glazed terra cotta tiles.

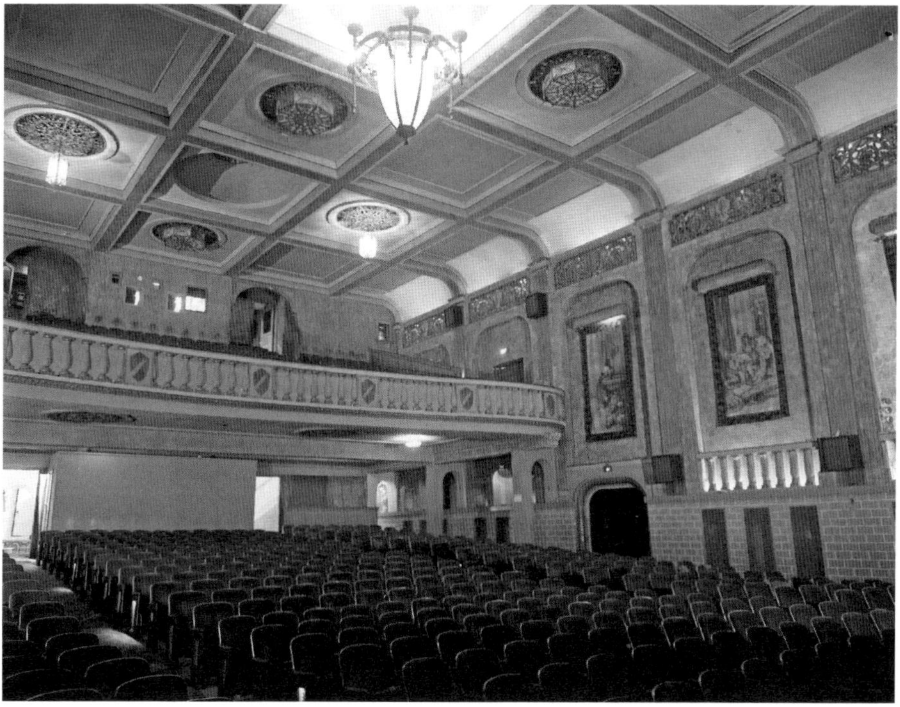

Even the interior of The Strand was remodeled in the elegance of the era. Other changes included refitting the theater for the silver screen.

the past. Interior changes were also made, and the theater could hold 593 people when it reopened. When silent films were recognized as something more than a passing fad, the theater was fitted out for their showing.

The dated exterior was addressed by the owners of The Strand when, in 1927, the theater was remodeled in the grandiose and elegant style of the theater palaces of the Ballaban and Katz tradition, by architect Henry J. Schneider. On the exterior, the façade was reconfigured and decorated using glazed terra cotta.

The Nonpareil Broadcasting Co. provided programs to area farmers. In 1947, radio studios for KSWI-FM—an anagram for the Key to Southwest Iowa–First FM station in the state—were installed on the top floor for broadcasting. Radio dramas, singers and bands all performed live in the spacious studios. By September, KSWI had become KFMX. Originally located on the mezzanine level, it offered a mix of live and prerecorded programs. The scarcity of FM radios forced the station off air in 1953 thanks to competition from television. Advertisers began to place their dollars in the

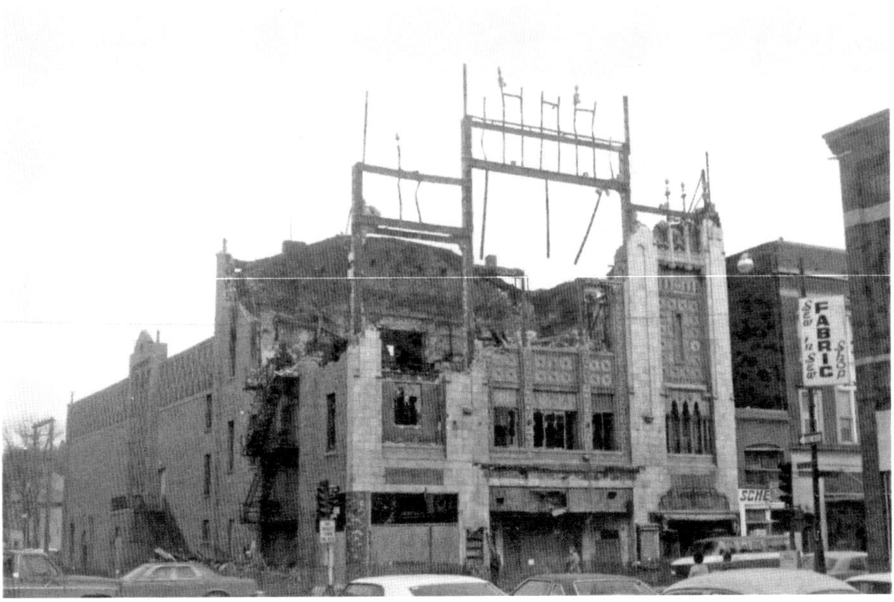

Following the last show on December 11, 1974, which no one attended, a fire damaged the building. It was razed shortly after for fear the façade would tumble into the street.

newer media. Even if you had a radio in your car or home, few had the ability to receive the FM band.

When the theater became part of the Fox Midwest Theaters from 1940 to '55, it was refitted for the wide screen. From 1955 to '64, it belonged to NTT Amusement, adding the screen to accommodate Cinemascope, and then reverted back to Fox in the 1970s. Finally, it returned to an independently owned theater when the Cohen family bought it. The decline in patrons took its toll on the old theater. Not all the films were G-rated. Some hard-core porn flashed across the screen, demeaning the theater and changing its clientele, making it hard for the theater to make a comeback with quality films.

On December 11, 1974, no one attended the film showing. That night, an electrical fire broke out. The fire burned through the front of the building. Though the building was not a total loss and could have been restored, instead it was razed, mostly because there wasn't sufficient business to justify keeping the theater open. The fragile façade also contributed to the need to tear down the structure.

VII

BUSINESSES AND BUILDINGS

The Kanesville Land Office opened in the spring of 1853 for the newly incorporated town of Council Bluffs. Some eighty-three thousand land warrants were issued to troops who had served in the conquest of New Mexico and California. The government issued warrants to soldiers as an incentive to settle the expanding nation.

The first three entries made in the land office were for Joseph B. Lane, Jacob Bush and Mrs. Marie Mynster on the north side of Indian Creek and what would become the Mynster Addition. In 1883, Marie was still dwelling there. After her husband's death, she sold the building to Mr. Harvey Kidney and Mr. Ira Platner, who opened the Ocean Wave saloon and built another home. The Watermill was one-third the length of Scott Street from Washington Avenue to where Bluff sloped to the west.

By 1855, taxes had finally been levied, and the city began improvements. Broadway was established at a uniform width instead of the meandering wide path it resembled. In 1833, the city offered sewer bonds for improvements and the laying of sewer lines at a cost of thirty-five dollars, with 6 percent interest paid out semiannually

A system of trollies was first put into service and drawn by mules. Light rail tracks were laid throughout downtown, and paving bricks were fitted around the rails. The trollies stopped at the major hotels in town and at the opera house. The tracks, in later years, were paved over with asphalt. Recently, the rails along Broadway were removed. In 1876, there were six miles of street railway, with early cars pulled by mules running along Broadway, Main and Pearl.

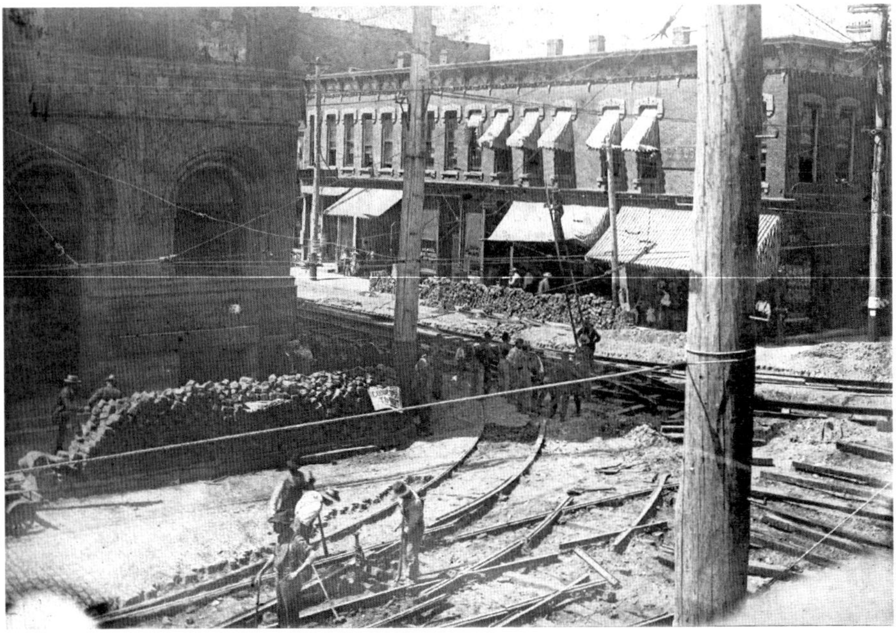

Workmen installing tracks at Broadway and Pearl. Council Bluffs was the second city in the nation to install an electric rail system.

A light rail transport system was put into service to move people from the city to the ferries, across the river to Omaha and back again. In 1868, mule cars were in use for transporting citizens. The Street Rail Road was licensed in early 1869 and completed by December. The line went down Broadway to the foot of the river to the ferry landing. It continued to be the western terminus of track until the railroad bridge over the Missouri River could be completed. The track then shifted to the transfer station of the Union Pacific Railroad. It was later replaced in 1872 by the Union Pacific "dummy" transportation lines.

Council Bluffs would be able to boast of being the second city in the nation to utilize the electric tram cars for its light rail system. Though the light rail was later replaced by buses, the public line remained an excellent mode of transportation for the citizens.

The railroad has been one of the most constant influences on Council Bluffs over the years. With the Transcontinental Railroad arriving in 1869, and the opening of the Union Pacific Missouri River Bridge in 1872, Council Bluffs became a major rail center. The Chicago and North Western Railroad came in 1867. Other railroads whose routes ran through the city included Rock Island and Pacific; Chicago Great Western; Wabash; Illinois Central; Chicago, Burlington and Quincy; Chicago, Milwaukee, St. Paul; and Pacific. In 1926, Carter Lake was formed form a change in the river's course. By the 1930s, Council Bluffs could boast of being the fifth-largest rail center in the nation.

The railroads kept Council Bluffs on the cutting edge. The city's principal streets were paved in 1884 with granite blocks. Cedar wood had previously been used to pave many streets to cut down on the mud. Gas lines were laid in 1870. A telephone service was established in Council Bluffs, with a general exchange in 1880. Another great change came on June 18, 1880, when the streets were renamed with numbered streets and avenues.

In 1876, Council Bluffs could boast of seventeen hotels, ten boardinghouses, three stockyards, three packing plants, four flour mills, four banks, nine public and church schools, twelve churches, three music halls, one opera house, twenty-six physicians, twenty-eight law firms, one brewery and thirty saloons. There are no listings given for the numerous houses of ill fame, but that is another story entirely.

A Driving Park for horse races thrived for many years, located at the north end of town. In the 1940s, Meyer Lansky operated a greyhound racing track.

A free public library was located on the third floor of the Merriam Block, taking up the entire north end of the building, with frontage on three streets giving a view on one side of the beautiful bluffs east of the city. The other side offered a view of Bayless Park, and the front gave a view of the business district. The large room was well lit by forty windows and handsome furnishings in old oak. The library had twenty-two thousand volumes with annual circulation of eighty-two thousand books. It also included a reference room with five thousand volumes and a reading room with newspapers and periodicals from as far away as San Francisco and New York, as well as some foreign magazines.

The library was first organized in March 1866 but was destroyed by fire in 1869. It was reorganized and incorporated again in 1871. It also served as the public school library. In 1878, the library building was described as being in a state of disrepair, ruin and decay. A library association was formed, and it added three thousand volumes. In 1881, a tax levy passed for new library; it opened to the public in 1882.

Over the years, many businesses have thrived and then passed into history. Some saw incredible success that reached from shore to shore; others floundered and left little mark on the city. We could fill another five books with the number of businesses and buildings lost. There are many businesses that have not been forgotten through the years, though they are no longer going concerns, and their once-proud edifices no longer grace the streets.

John G. Woodward & Co.

The John G. Woodward Candy Company is one of the most beloved and fondly remembered businesses in Council Bluffs. Before it was the Woodward Candy Company, it had been the candy firm of Duquett & Company, which made a general line of candies in the Mynster Building on West Broadway. When Duquett sold to Woodward, the business soon needed more room, and in 1895, Woodward built the first of many expansions at 211 West Broadway. It had a warehouse at 901 South Eighth Street.

The design of the factory building was created by Chris Jensin, a Danish architect. In 1899 and 1907, the plant was expanded to keep up with demand. In 1907, some two to three hundred people were employed in the factory, and a team of twelve to fifteen salesmen sold the products on the road to stores around the country. At the height of its tenure, the factory

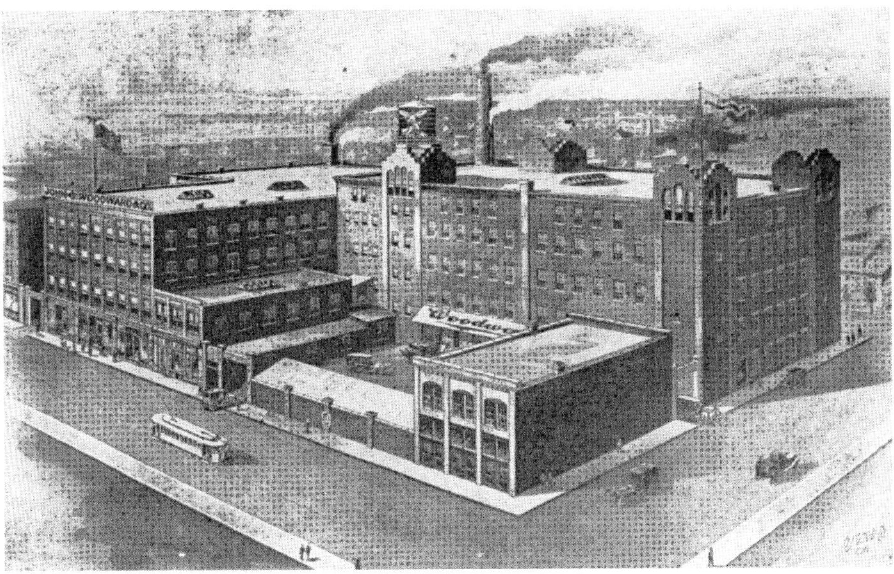

John G. Woodward & Co. at 211 West Broadway employed five hundred workers and twenty-five salesmen who sold their goods from the Atlantic to the Pacific.

employed five hundred workers and twenty-five traveling salesmen who had territory that spanned the nation from coast to coast.

Woodward sunk an artesian well down to more than eight hundred feet and found an abundant supply of fresh water that was used in making its candies. Maybe this was the secret ingredient that gave the candy such a wonderful flavor. The company also bottled and sold the water, and these sales became a large part of its extensive business. It sold the carbonated water, claiming it possessed medicinal purposes, under the name of Deborah Mineral Springs Lithia Water. Woodward also bottled and sold ginger ale.

From atop the factory, the iconic water tower looked out over the city. It served a practical purpose in that it was always kept full and was there in the case a fire broke out. The water stored there could flood the entire plant and douse any flames.

By the 1930s, Woodward delivered its products to thirty-nine states and made 3.5 million pounds of candy a year. Inez and Jean Bergant, a pair of little people, worked in the family grocery, and Woodward asked if they would be its spokespersons for the candies in advertising campaigns. They gladly accepted the offer. Mr. and Mrs. Bergant were for many years the faces for Woodward Candy Company; their photographs were used in advertisements nationwide. Inez and Jean built a special house located at 517 Fourth Street in Council Bluffs to accommodate their diminutive size.

According to the census of 1900, the Woodward family resided at 919 Sixth Avenue in Council Bluffs. In 1905, Mr. Woodward purchased a home at 370 Oakland Avenue. When John Woodward died in 1936, his son Carleton wasn't interested in continuing in the candy business. He sold off a number of the original recipes to Russell Stover. The trademark was sold to Fenn Brothers of Sioux City, South Dakota, and according to an article in the *New York Times* on December 28, 1938, the Woodward Candy Company manufacturing facilities were sold to Union Standard of New York. Union Standard had no intentions of keeping the factory in Council Bluffs open.

The Hinky Dinky grocery store took a lease on the old Woodward Candy Company building. It remodeled part of the offices and tore down other sections. In 1955, it offered the first rooftop parking to it patrons. In 1970, the grocery store moved to Bluff Plaza and sublet the leased building to Ranks after the Ranks store building was destroyed by a horrible fire. People gathered in the streets, watching the building burn. When the fire reached the ammunition in the building, reports of exploding bullets echoed along Broadway.

Eventually, the property was purchased under the auspices of the Council Bluffs renewal plan and torn down to make way for a strip shopping mall.

John Beno & Co.

Born in 1845 in Alsace, France, now a part of Germany, John Beno arrived in Council Bluffs in the spring of 1861 with his brother. He worked in a local express office in 1863. Then he worked in the J.L. Foreman store as a salesman. In the spring of 1866, Mr. Foreman closed his business. John Beno then worked as a salesman for Johnson, Spratt & Co. for a year.

After that, Beno formed a partnership with Foreman, creating the concern of Foreman & Beno. This partnership lasted until August 1879, when Beno withdrew to travel to Oregon to visit family. In 1880, John Beno returned to Council Bluffs and opened a general merchandise store at 18 Main and 17 Pearl Streets. It was a two-story building with general goods on the ground floor and clothing and store rooms on the second floor. The business started out small but grew quickly. He invited his nephews to come into the business with him.

Simon and Henry Eisman of Germany came to Council Bluffs in 1861 and opened Henry Eisman & Co. clothing, a wholesale clothing establishment. Their ads touted their success as having started out small, but they could

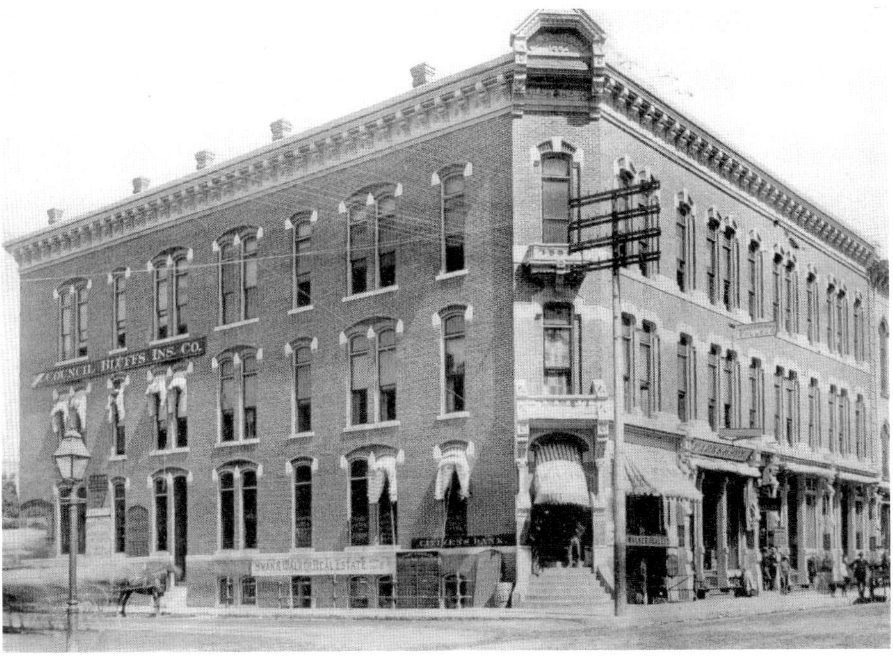

A mark of success was to build a large, modern building. The Shugart Beno Block stood until a fire ravaged the building.

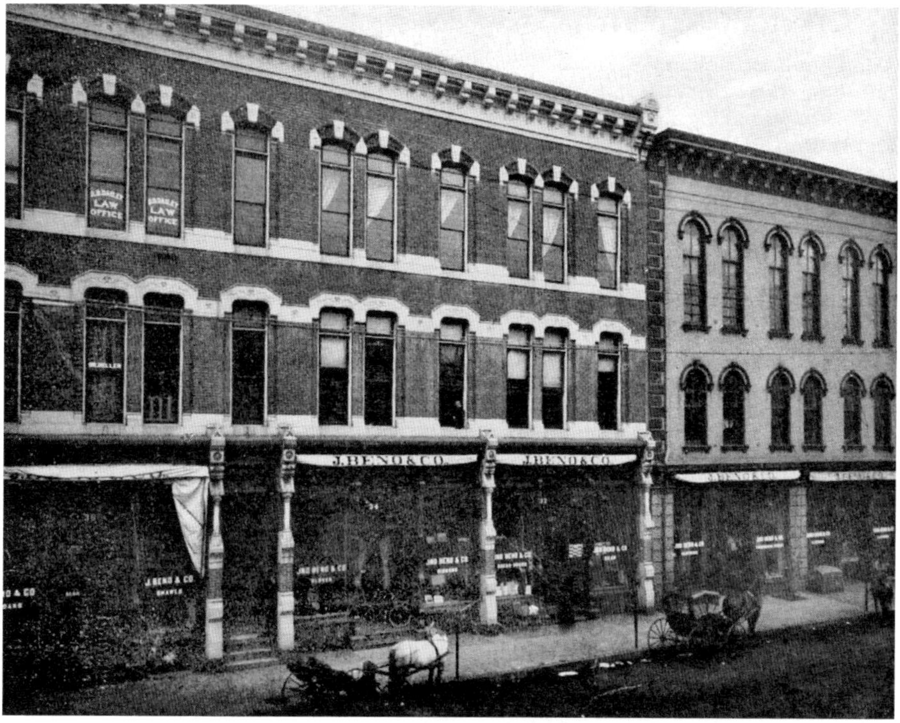

Above Beno's store at 18 Main and 17 Pearl Streets. The business grew, and a larger building was soon needed to house the wide selection of goods.

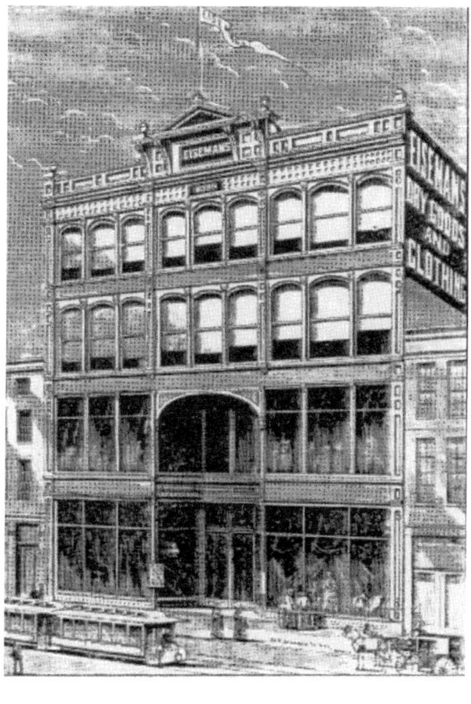

Right: The Eisman Block, with skylights and the Western College on the top floor. John Beno & Co. purchased this building in 1900.

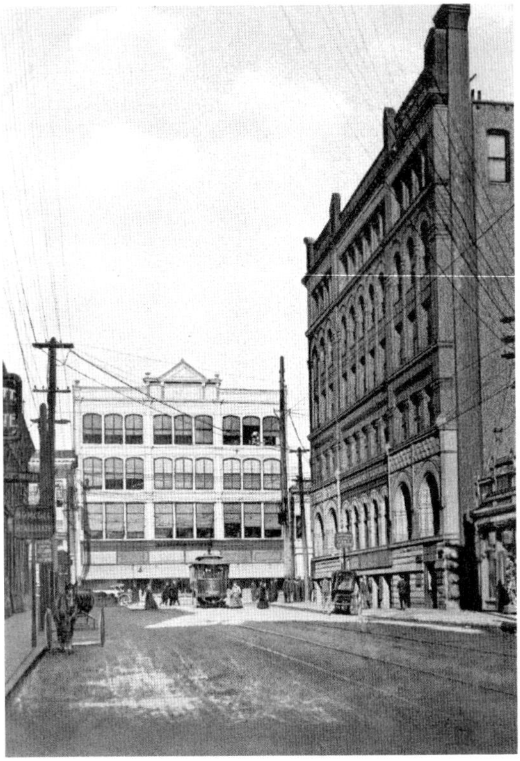

Left: The Eisman Building at the foot of Pearl. Beno's bought it and took over the entire building for its merchandise.

Below: On August 26, 1904, the Missouri River flooded. Before the levees were built, the river would periodically breach its banks.

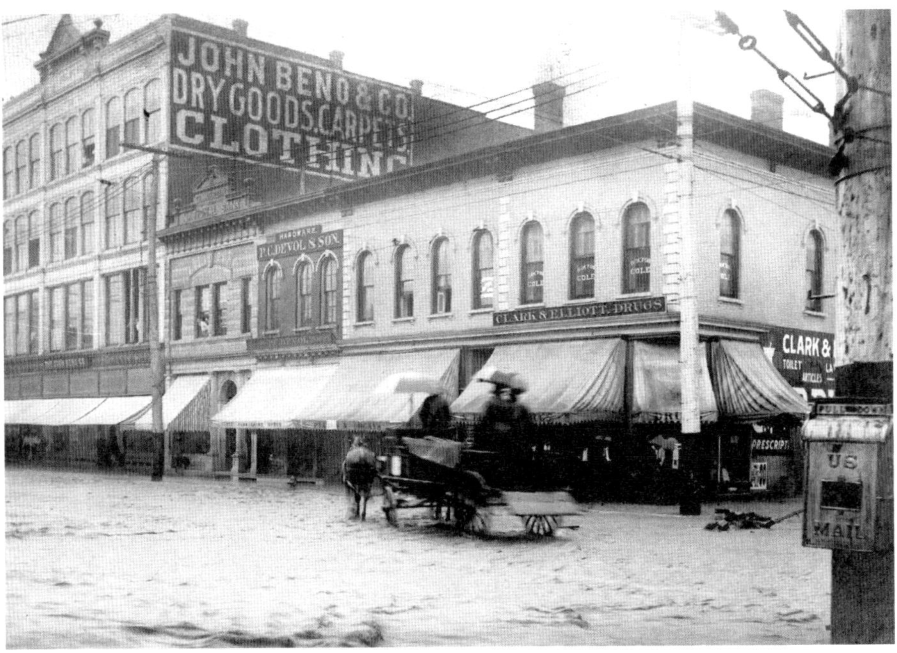

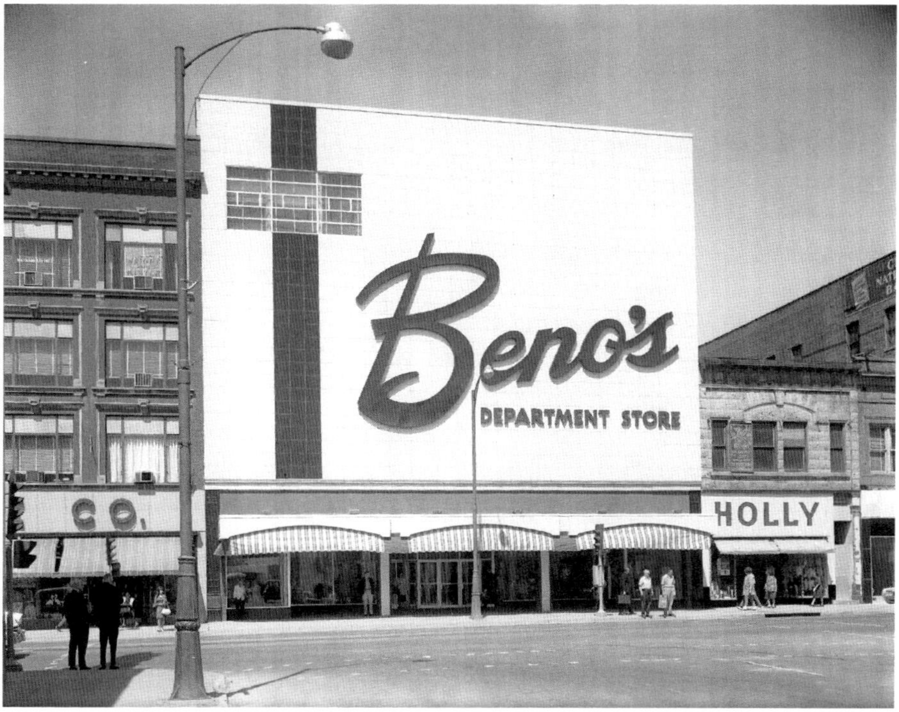

Beno's in the early 1970s, with its modern façade, as many stores attempted to give a fresh look to their businesses.

soon boast of larger sales than any other house in Iowa: $100,000 average value of goods in stock and annual sales at nearly $4,250,000, with twelve to fifteen employees.

Soon Beno & Co. had to move to larger quarters, opposite the Grand Hotel, to keep up with demand. He occupied five adjoining stores of three levels each. Beno's soon outgrew this space, and in 1900, it purchased the Eisman Building, already known for a fine selection of clothing, at 516 Broadway at the foot of Pearl. Over the years, the building underwent a number of facelifts and interior changes.

Beno established the largest department store in the state with an extensive variety of stock and employed fifty people. He sold his interests to his nephews when he discovered he had cancer. He died on June 13, 1907.

Beno's at 516 West Broadway sat empty when the store moved into Midlands Mall in 1973. The old Beno's store building was razed to make room for urban renewal.

Masonic Temple

On June 8, 1855, the Grand Lodge granted dispensation for Bluff City Lodge #71. The first meeting occurred on July 21, 1855, at the Odd Fellow's Hall, a two-story frame building on Stutsman Street.

They later moved to more comfortable accommodations, and on June 8, 1856, their charter was granted. They met on the third floor of the old Empire Block at Pearl and Broadway. As the lodge grew, more space was needed. They refitted their lodge by enlarging it fifteen feet and laying Brussels carpeting; new stations were purchased, and desks and other furniture were repainted and varnished. The front part of the building served as anterooms.

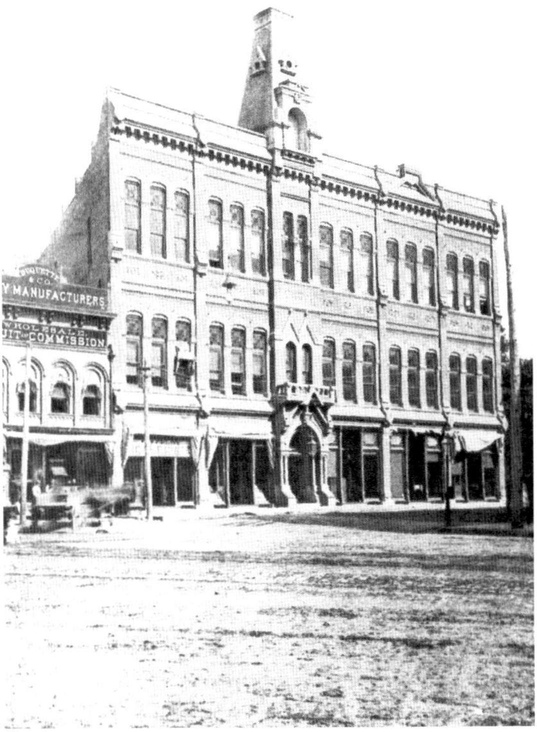

The Masonic temple at the junction of Fourth and Broadway. It was a grand edifice that towered over the neighboring buildings one hundred feet from sidewalk to the tower.

On June 27, 1883, discussions for a larger hall began to be reported in the *Nonpareil*. On July 15, 1883, there were calls for architectural plans to be submitted, with estimated costs of $20,000. Approval was granted for the removal of buildings on the site where the Odd Fellows chose to build: the junction of Broadway and Fourth, with a sixty-foot frontage and one hundred feet deep. The first story would have sixteen-foot-high ceilings, and the second and third would have eighteen-foot-high ceilings. The second floor, with the use of trusses, would have a large hall clear of all obstructions. The floors would be "deadened" so that sound wouldn't carry from above or below. The ceiling in the lodge would be twenty feet high. The cornerstone was laid on July 20, 1883, and hopes of completion and occupancy were projected for January 1884.

By January 9, 1884, the *Nonpareil* was reporting progress on the building of the most beautiful Masonic Hall in the West. Foundations were begun in mid-September, and the cornerstone was laid with all due ceremony on October 5, 1884. The frontage of the building would be 105 feet at 100 feet deep. It would be three stories but have the height of four stories due to its interior ceilings. For the trusses, an extra 5 feet would be necessary between the second and third floors. The firewalls would make the building 68 feet from the sidewalk to the top and 100 feet from the sidewalk to top of the tower.

The first floor was dedicated to merchants' purposes; the north portion of the second floor to offices; and the south part fitted up as a hall for lectures, concerts, sociable, festivals, club dances and so on. This hall was sixty feet wide and one hundred feet deep, with eighteen-foot-high ceilings. Also, there was an ample stage with dressing rooms. All columns and pillars were entirely avoided by having the floor above supported by trusses—all at great expense. Off this hall was a kitchen. The building was heated by steam and fitted with gas, water and all other modern improvements for the comfort and convenience of the occupants. The dedication was held on December 18, 1884. Throughout the following years, grand parties, balls and celebrations were held in this commodious hall.

The police held their newly instituted policeman's ball in the large hall in the Masonic Temple on November 1, 1937. The fourth annual policeman's ball was held in 1934 at the Civic Auditorium, with a banquet at the Chieftain Hotel; 2,500 people attended.

Like so many buildings that go out of fashion, their architecture looks dated, and people seek newer, more modern structures. The Masonic Hall was put up for sale. A new Masonic temple replaced the old one in 1961, located at 130 South Sixth Street. The elegant old Masonic Hall was demolished in 1973. Up on the third floor, rooms that housed the Masons' meetings still retained their original décor.

J.F. Wilcox, Florist

The highly successful business of Mr. J.F. Wilcox and Sons had its origins in 1867, when L.A. and Mary Casper farmed land east of Council Bluffs. Mary began to put up the abundance from her garden. She began to sell her

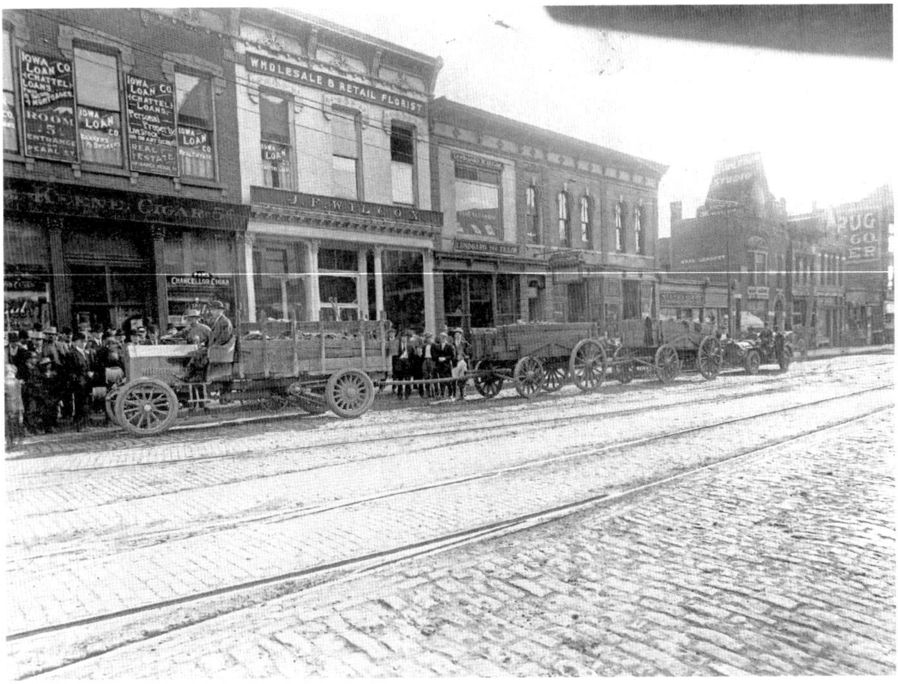

J.F. Wilcox, at 521 Broadway. Wilcox worked for his uncle L.A. Casper before buying him out and building one of the largest floral businesses in the nation.

canned goods, and her husband, seeing this was a success, built her a few lean-to greenhouses. He soon joined her in her gardening, and their success grew.

John F. Wilcox came to work for Mr. Casper as a laborer. In 1885, John married Mr. Casper's niece, Emma. He saved his earnings and bought into the business. It continued to flourish. Mr. Caspar had expanded to include flowers grown in the greenhouses. The original site of the greenhouses was located on North Avenue. In the 1870s, Mr. Casper opened his florist shop in Council Bluffs. The business enjoyed a growing patronage and expanded steadily over the years.

In 1892, Mr. Casper retired and sold out to his nephew John Franklin Wilcox. He placed his own name on the door, and under his management the modest floral business grew to mammoth proportions. He built his own greenhouses, utilizing 425,000 square feet of glass and miles of piping to regulate the inside temperatures in the colder months of the year. The plant used five thousand tons of coal to maintain the proper warmth inside the greenhouses.

Wilcox & Sons became a continental supplier of flowers, with 750,000 square feet dedicated to the growing of poinsettias, roses, chrysanthemums,

Easter lilies, daffodils, geraniums and more. Orders came from New York to Seattle and from St. Louis to Minneapolis. So successful was the floral aspect that Mr. Wilcox also opened an establishment to furnish fresh vegetables for all seasons. His concern, at one time, was the largest in the nation.

The storefront was located at 521 Broadway, and in 1904, Mr. Wilcox built a fine large home near the greenhouses at 1132 East Pierce Street. He also began operation at Manawa. Later, the retail shop operated from 28 Pearl Street.

In May 1912, John F. Wilcox was taken ill. Eleven days later, he died of pneumonia. His eldest son, Roy Franklin Wilcox, stepped in to carry on the business. All of his brothers were still in school at the time. All his sons followed their father in the successful business. Blaine Caspar became an important part of the management of the business until his ill health forced him to retire in 1954. At that time, they closed the retail store, but the company continued to supply flowers all over the country. Blaine died in 1960 at age sixty-three. He was living at the family home his father built.

The next generation continued the business until 1990, when Bloomin John's, located in the Midland's Mall, closed. The business had been run by John Wilcox's grandson Donald and his nephews Bob and John.

One of those horrendous hail storms that periodically hit the area dropped hen-sized hailstones on August 30, 1956. Over five thousand panes of glass in the Wilcox greenhouses were shattered.

The elegant mansion—which many notable people, such as President Teddy Roosevelt, visited—was torn down in 1967 to make way for the new Highway 6. Wilcox used one million square feet of glass in covering over twenty acres of greenhouses. In October 1970, the greenhouses on North Avenue and Highway 6 were razed. The home and other greenhouses were also demolished. Today, it is the site of the Kirn Junior High School.

Merriam Block

Nathan Merriam built his four-story office building at Willow between Main and Pearl Streets in 1889, designed by the architectural firm of Allen & Bell. There were eight large stores on the first floor and at least forty-two offices on upper floors. The building spanned from Main to Pearl with a two-hundred-foot frontage on each street. Council Bluffs pressed bricks were used in the construction.

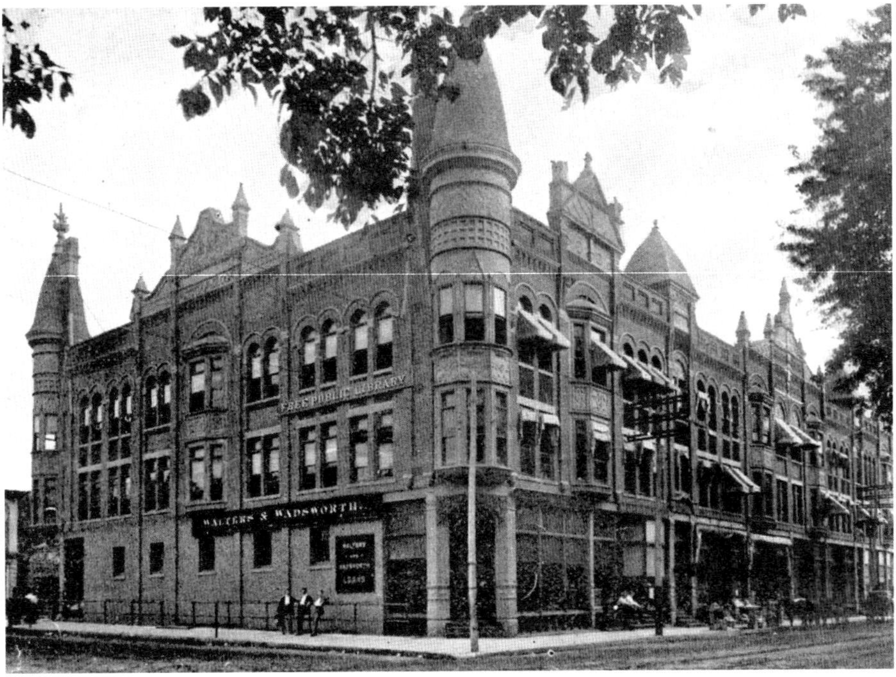

Merriam Block spanned between Pearl and Main Streets. The Mabray gang rented offices and ran the largest con ever pulled off in the nation's history.

The Merriam Block opened on July 26, 1889, with music rendered by Dalbey's Orchestra, and the ladies of the Episcopal church served refreshments. Thousands turned out to see the latest building in a grand collection of fine buildings that graced the city.

Available spaces filled steadily. A free public library with twelve thousand volumes occupied a large section of the third floor with windows on the three sides affording plenty of natural light to readers. Also located on third floor was the board of trade, the YMCA, the Wabash railroad offices and the WCTU (Woman's Christian Temperance Union). The second floor filled quickly with seven lawyers, a number of architects, opticians, insurance agents and real estate offices. The first floor was seen as a prime location for any store and filled quickly as well.

A darker side of the history of the building came in the name of John Mabray and his gang of con men. One of the largest gambling schemes ever to have existed found its headquarters in offices in the Merriam Block. The staggering amounts of cash swindled from unsuspecting men across the nation rivaled the criminal activities of even Charles Ponzi and Bernard

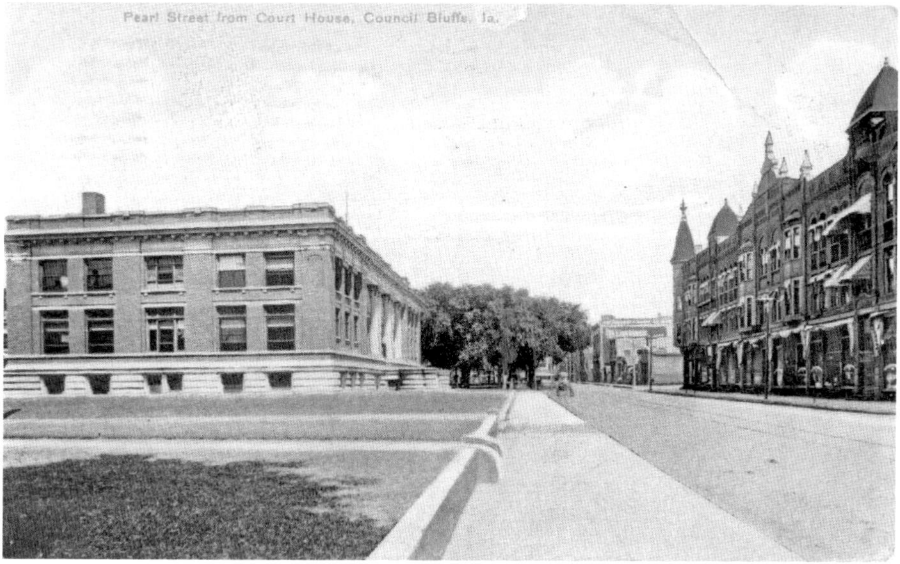

The Meriam Block was razed in 1938. By 1940, the new city hall, police station and jail had replaced it.

Madoff and the savings and loan scandal of Michael Milken. In today's money, the takings would be in the multiple billions of dollars.

The Mabray gang moved their headquarters to Council Bluffs, as the authorities were becoming aware of their activities in another city.

The John C. Mabray gang, also known as the Millionaires' Club, had a nationwide network of con men working in cities across the country: New Orleans, Denver, Council Bluffs and points in between. The fake sporting events were so well planned that victims never suspected they were being taken. Some of the victims joined with the swindlers, enlisting other gullible, greedy men in hopes of getting back some of their lost money. Losses ran from $2,000 all the way up to nearly $40,000 per victim—depending on the willingness of the mark to contribute to the fraud.

The Mabray gang had fourteen branches in various locations about the country, but all con men now operated from Council Bluffs. Foot racing, wrestling, prizefighting, horse racing and wire tapping were the ways operatives would entice victims to make some easy money.

The victim was usually approached by a friend who had, himself, been solicited previously by a man called a steerer to bring in business. The setup sounds right out of the film *The Sting*. The steerer would claim to have a cousin who was a secretary to a number of very wealthy men who did as they pleased, traveling for pleasure. The man would comment that the secretary was angry at some ill treatment and planned to swindle the wealthy men out of a large amount of money utilizing their own game. The victim was asked if he wanted to help. This is how the mark was lured to the first swindle.

The cons were simple and well executed. They would be pulled off at various places around the country. The gang set up fake matches using a supposed champion in either wrestling or boxing who was to spar with an opponent. With a big buildup of the champion's easy chances at winning, the mark was induced to bet on the champ. The fight began, and everything looked like the champ would beat his opponent easily and the winnings were a sure thing. The victim could almost taste the cash. Then, at a crucial moment, everything that could go wrong did. The underdog opponent would manage to get the champ into a stranglehold. That's when blood would suddenly begin to gush out of the champ's mouth. It appeared to all present that that the easy favorite was suffering a fatal hemorrhage.

This is when part two of the con went into effect. One of Mabray's men would hurry the victim out of the area, filling him with the fear of arrest because he'd been gambling illegally. When the police came, as surely they would, the victim would be arrested. He was gotten out of there as fast as they could get him to move. He had lost his bet when the fight ended in tragedy. Mabray's man knew the mark would keep quiet.

They were able to pull off this fake hemorrhage with the use of chicken blood held in a small, bladder-like pocket made from the entrails of a sheep. This was held in the mouth of the favorite through a few rounds until that predetermined moment when he would break it open with his teeth and appear to be bleeding. For extra added effect, the champion would fall to the ground and writhe as if in agony.

Later, the con man would meet up with the mark and offer to help him get his money back. The mark often would head back home, getting all his ready cash—selling, mortgaging or taking a loan to amass as much as he could—and then return to the con man ready to win the next "sure thing."

Men starting out for a bit of sport with hopes of easy money ended up losing nearly everything they had.

Another legend of the shadier side of Council Bluff's past had a relationship to the Mabray gang. Ben Marks ran a notorious gambling establishment with plenty of soiled doves to satisfy any sporting man's needs. Marks had a race track out at Lake Manawa that was a playground for the people of the area and tourists who delighted in the lake and its amenities. Some of Mark's races at Manawa were layered with hype and the smokescreen of grandiose showmanship that goes hand in hand with fakery and fixing a race. Much like the staged fights, the jockey would push his horse to win, and everything looked like it would be a sure thing. The jockey would then break open the bladder of blood in his mouth as he fell from his horse. It paid well for a while, but soon enough the trickery was revealed.

What brought it all to an end was a misdirected letter. A postal clerk placed an envelope in the wrong post box, thus setting in motion an investigation that would topple the entire racket. The misdirected letter was dated March 1, 1908, and brought down the infamous Mabray gambling syndicate. The letter read:

> *Friend 39:*
> *Owing to a change of administration here, we move to Council Bluffs, Iowa where conditions are perfect.*
> *Drop us a line and keep us posted as to your whereabouts.*
> *With best wishes,*
> *"753"*
> *Will be ready for business by March 15.*

When Mabray was arrested, authorities located a trunk in his home that contained complete records of all transactions spanning a four-year period. A loose-leaf pocket ledger contained the names and addresses of some two hundred men who had acted as go-betweens, the men who would help secure the next mark. These men lived all over the country.

Mabray had built up quite a sinister and exceedingly powerful influence; he had police, sheriff's officers and other authorities under his control, thereby managing to thwart any attempt to bring him to justice, at least until the U.S. Postal Inspection Service managed to end his unbridled reign of greed. In June 1908, the first arrests were made. U.S. postal authorities indicted eighty-seven members of the gang. The newspapers carried the story all across the nation as more and more arrests were made.

In 1937, the Merriam Block was razed to make room for the new city hall. In December 1937, the building and land were purchased for $21,000.

Banking Houses

From the mid-1800s, banking houses have been a part of the city's growth and prosperity. In 1873, there were four banking houses in Council Bluffs:

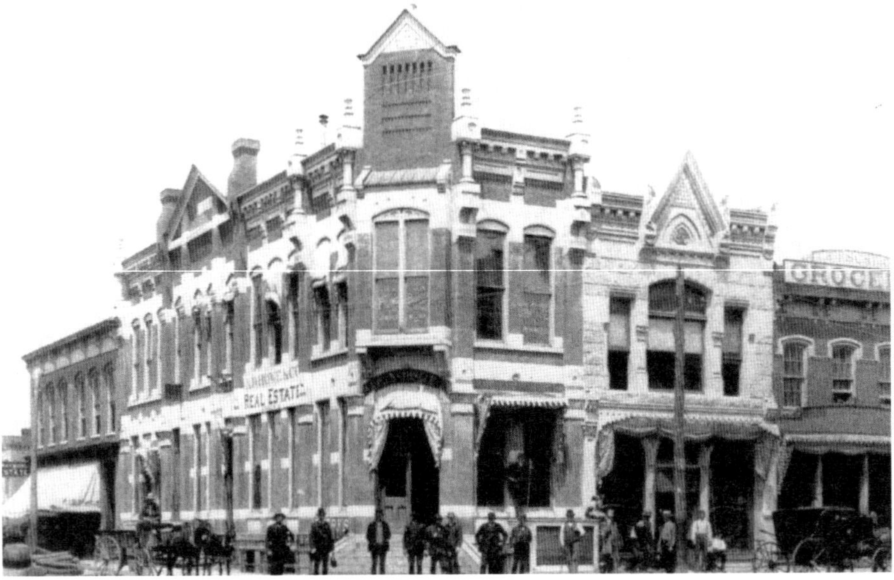

The State Savings Bank was located in the Kimball and Champ Building in the 1890s, located on the northeast corner of West Broadway and Main Streets.

First National, Pacific National, Council Bluffs Savings Bank and the banking house of Officer and Pusey.

In Illinois, Thomas Pusey married Elizabeth Officer, thus beginning a partnership that was to have a great influence on Council Bluff City. When the married couple visited Robert and Margaret Officer's home, they met a reticent young lawyer who had, like Mr. Officer, been a surveyor in Illinois. This man would one day ascend to the highest office in the nation. His name was Abraham Lincoln. The friendship between Abraham Lincoln and the Pusey and Officer families would continue for many years. William Pusey and Thomas Officer joined together in forming their banking house in Council Bluffs in 1853.

Thomas Officer died in 1890.

When Mr. W.H.M. Pusey died on November 15, 1900, at the asylum in Clarinda, an interesting story ran in the *Nonpareil*:

> *Nothing could have caused more astonishment then the closing of the banking house of Officer and Pusey. The first breath of suspicion that there might be something wrong, longtime friends rejected the idea. Mr. Pusey had always been conservative in his business practices, plain, even frugal in his habits and possessed an almost severe piety that no one ever suspected that he had a million in the vault.*

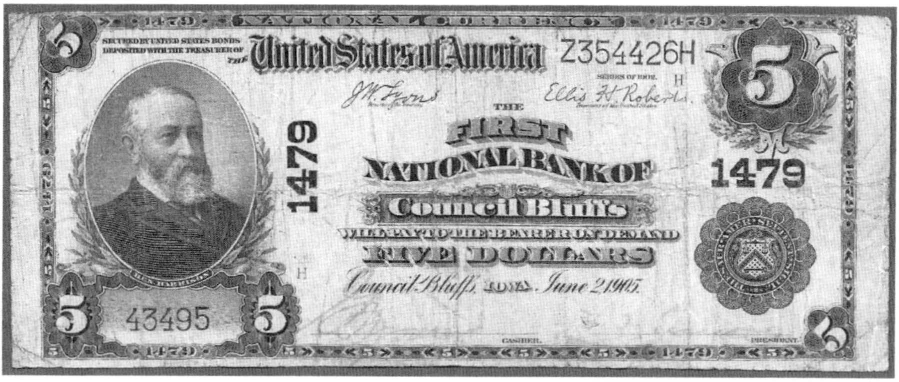

Above: A 1905 bank note minted by the First National Bank of Council Bluffs.

Right: The Council Bluffs Savings Bank, a downtown landmark at the intersection of Broadway and Pearl, where the trolleys intersected.

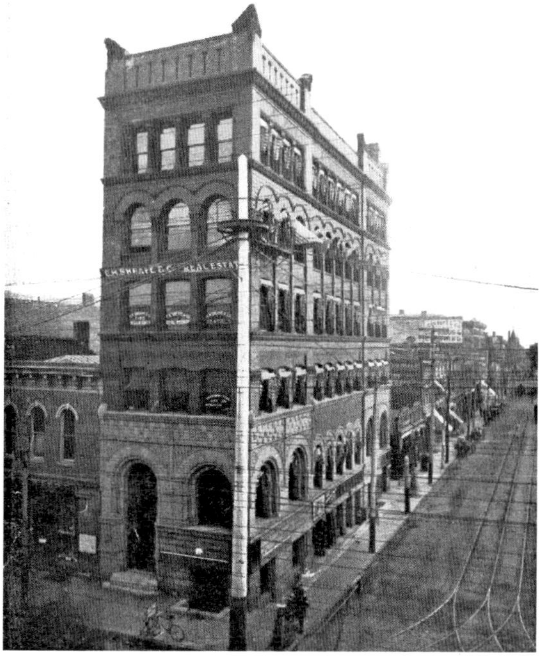

On August 5, 1872, $20,000 in currency was stolen from the First National Bank. The robbers may have entered the bank by a side door that led to Main Street, through the alcove in the bank and from there to the vault door. No one was seen or heard. The robbers were able to abscond with the cash from the safe. No trace of the money was ever found.

There was a monetary panic in 1873 caused by a collapse of the banks as a result of making poor real estate loans. This had repercussions for the city. Council Bluffs suspended all improvements, the real estate market became stagnant and grasshoppers devastated great swaths of farmland. The hard times pressed down, especially on the poor and those dependent on labor to earn their livings.

Newspapers

Newspapers are the lifeline to the history of any town; they record the events that may pass as insignificant to us. Sometimes the old papers reveal secrets that have been pushed under the rug, for they may have been seen as embarrassing as history was written and rewritten. The papers relate the events that have shaped the city for better or worse: the opening of new businesses, the closing of once-thriving concerns, who of import has died and who has slipped away unnoticed. Newspapers relate the struggles with crime, the horrors of devastating fires and the march of progress as the wrecking ball razes the past. Some columns even relate who was visiting in town and whom they had come to see. This has passed out of style as cities have grown and that news isn't so easy to track down.

Council Bluffs has been fortunate to have any number of newspapers recording the growth and history of the city since the late 1840s. Many newspapers have published, thrived and failed through the years. The most tenacious has been the *Nonpareil.* Of all the papers that have informed readers through the decades, this paper alone has stood the test of time and still publishes a daily newspaper. In keeping with the changing demands of contemporary times, the *Nonpareil* has accommodated the present-day reader with an electronic version of the paper.

The first paper published in the city was the *Frontier Guardian*, established in 1848 by Orson Hyde. He took a portion of this printing equipment west when he migrated to Utah, leaving the rest behind. Mr. Babbitt put the abandoned equipment to use for the *Bugle*. The offices of the *Frontier Guardian* became the central location to which all other businesses related their location. In advertisements in the newspapers, businesses located themselves as "three doors west of the newspaper office," "across the street" and so on. When Orson Hyde departed for Utah, the *Frontier Guardian* was absorbed into the *Bugle*.

The *Weekly Bugle* was founded in 1850 by Almon W. Babbitt. It sat on the north side of Broadway, four rods west of the street, near Indian Creek. In 1857, Babbitt expanded from weekly publication and printed the *Daily Bugle*. After A.W. Babbitt's mysterious death, supposedly at the hands of Indians, the *Bugle* passed into the hands of Joseph Johnson. Both the *Frontier Guardian* and the

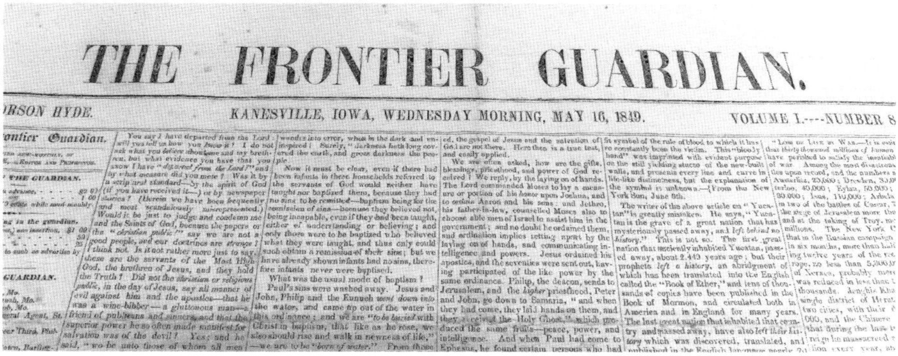

THE FRONTIER GUARDIAN.

ORSON HYDE. KANESVILLE, IOWA, WEDNESDAY MORNING, MAY 16, 1849. VOLUME I.----NUMBER 8

In 1848, the *Frontier Guardian* was the first paper published by Orson Hyde. The newspaper's offices were the central hub; all business related their locations to its offices.

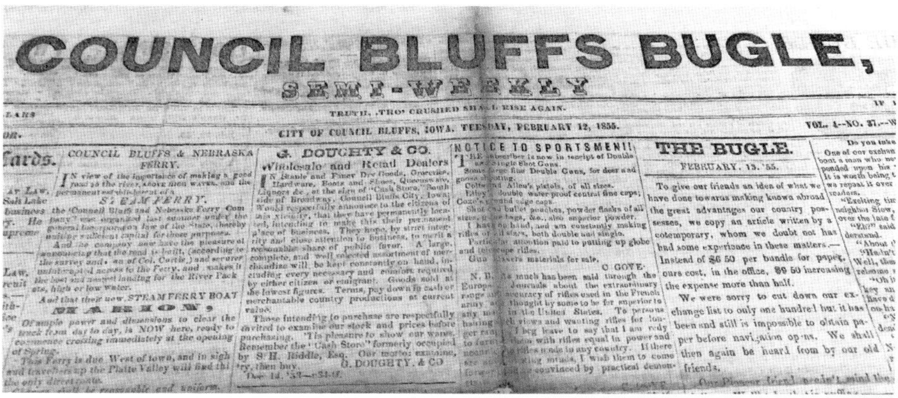

COUNCIL BLUFFS BUGLE,

SEMI-WEEKLY

TRUTH, THO' CRUSHED SHALL RISE AGAIN.

CITY OF COUNCIL BLUFFS, IOWA. TUESDAY, FEBRUARY 12, 1855. VOL. 4--NO. 37.

Almon Babbitt established the *Bugle*. When Hyde departed for Utah, the *Bugle* absorbed the *Guardian*, flourishing until it was succeeded by the *Council Bluffs Times*.

Bugle were Mormon papers, but they presented opposing views. In 1870, the *Bugle* was succeeded by the *Council Bluffs Times*, which lasted until 1871.

Over the years, many newspapers have begun, flourished, changed hands, come under new management and perished. Some left little record behind, but some we are fortunate enough to have a great number of issues preserved. What follows are just some of the many newspapers that the citizens of Council Bluffs read through the years. This list is incomplete; to give an accurate and complete listing is no easy task, as so many newspapers have come and gone through the years.

In 1854, Jerimiah Folsom established the *Chronotype*, a Whig paper. The Whig Party was the precursor to the Republican Party. Later, it became a Democratic paper, renamed the *Democratic Clarion*.

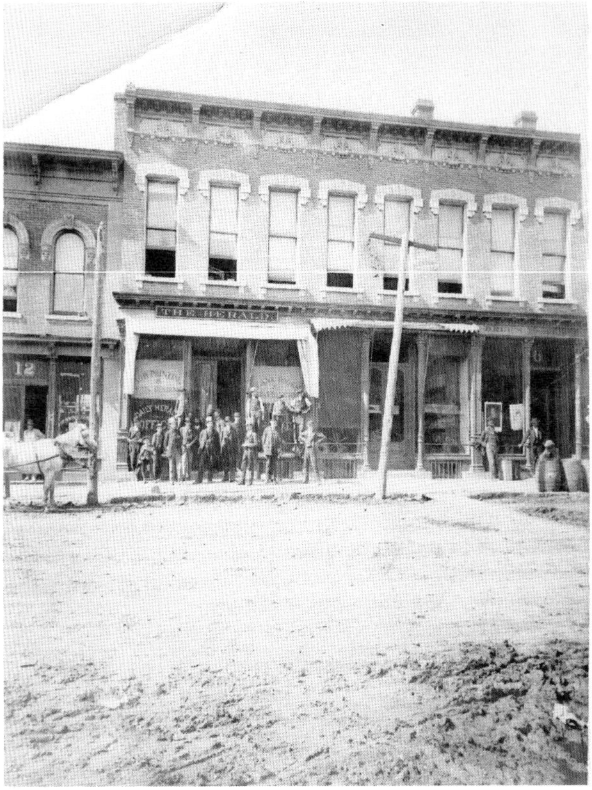

Left: Men in front of the *Herald*, at 10 Pearl Street. Next door at 12 Pearl Street, a man stands in the doorway of the *Daily Globe*.

Below: The *Nonpareil* is the only paper to have survived the test of time. It moved from this building into a new modern building on Broadway.

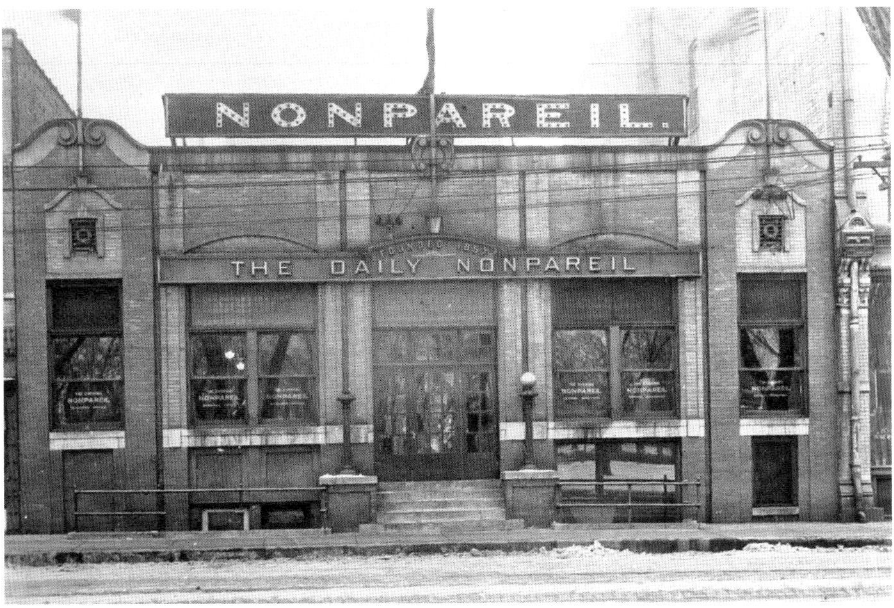

In 1859, J.E. Johnson established a Democratic paper, the *Council Bluffs Press*.

The Empire Block, built in 1855, was the first three-story brick building to be erected in town. It sat on the south side of Broadway between Main and Pearl. In the spring of 1857, W.W. Maynard and Henry De Long established the *Weekly Nonpareil*. Another family to arrive and put down roots was the Bloomer family, building a wooden-frame home at 123 Fourth Street. In 1856, Bloomer helped found the Episcopal Church.

In 1857, another newspaper opened: the *Nonpareil*. William Wirt Maynard bought a printing press in St. Louis and had it shipped by steamboat to Wray's Landing. This was the latest in printing presses: a Wells Celebrated Power Press. The power source was steam. The first issue of the *Nonpareil* came out on May 2, 1857. It boasted four pages with eight columns, twenty-three inches deep. It was published every Saturday morning in the number one Palmer Block, at Broadway and Scott, on the third floor for a subscription of two dollars per year. The paper was located in this building at the time it caught fire, on June 24, 1867. The newspaper lost all its type and press—it was a total loss. The Young Men's Library was also in the building, and it was totally destroyed. The block was leveled by the fire.

The first German-language newspaper, *Freie Presse*, was established by Mr. Wenbore and Worden and first printed in 1867 in Council Bluffs. Also in 1867, W.T. Gibbs began a German Democratic paper: the *Council Bluffs Presse*. By 1875, Mr. F.G. Pfeiffer of Oregon had settled in Council Bluff City and purchased the *Freie Presse*, which gained in popularity through the 1880s and '90s. In 1899, Alois Becher purchased the paper and published it at 512 South Main. The paper was sold about 1914.

In November 1871, the *Globe Democrat*, started by S.W. Morehead, opened. In 1872, Jacob Williams became editor. By 1879, Mr. Morgan had bought a half interest in the newspaper.

In the early 1880s, the *Evening Herald* began. This was a prohibition paper. After a short run, it was succeeded by the *Independent Republican*. The *Herald* was published from 1883 to 1884. The building was located at 10 Pearl Street, next door to the *Daily Globe*. The paper continued until 1900. In May 1868, the *Council Bluffs Democrat* published both a daily and weekly paper. The newspaper didn't last long; on October 1, 1868, the last "red hot" issue rolled off the presses with a number of bitter, denunciatory articles.

VIII

URBAN RENEWAL

From the fledgling settlement of tents and log buildings, Council Bluffs has endured many challenges. Fires and floods have taken their toll, allowing the city to rebuild and start anew. Yet only one thing wiped away the older buildings of a huge swath of downtown in one fell swoop. Sections of a block might be lost to raging fires, floods might weaken foundations, age might collapse a building, but nothing compares to the level of destruction wreaked on the city in the 1970s under the guise of urban renewal.

The buildings of downtown stood for many years, side by side, aging gracefully—some better than others. Facelifts revitalized an older look with something more modern. But these businesses were familiar friends that citizens knew well and supported with their patronage.

In 1976, the Midlands Mall destroyed the downtown.

The promise in 1973 of federally funded grants to revitalize an aging downtown caught the interest of some people in the city. It took an urban renewal grant to decimate most of the historic downtown. Someone remembered a remark made by the man in charge of the destruction to come.

In preparing for this book, people shared memories; they poured out of them freely and with joy.

We see an old photograph of how the city used to be before the vast change swept it all away. The photo stirs old memories, bringing back those days of our youth, simpler times—times of learning, exploring, of first loves and family members gathered about. One could close her eyes and remember that past. Recalling the sights, sounds and smells of the past, these senses stir memories

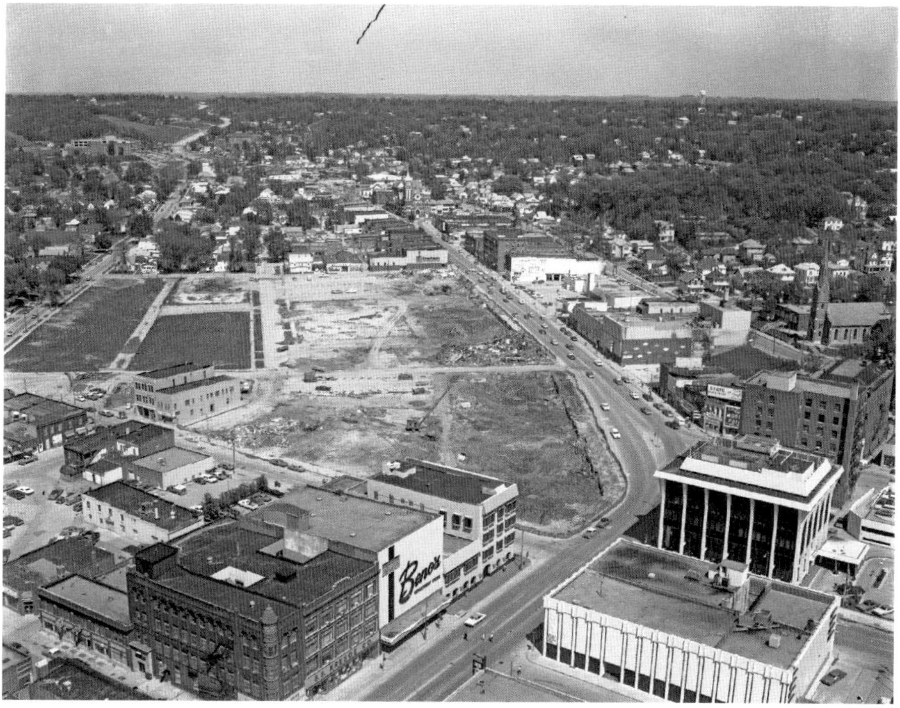

The urban renewal of 1973, looking down Broadway—clearing downtown in preparation for the mall.

stored away and lovingly experienced again. The sound of our footfalls on the aging boards of Beno's, the whoosh of the cartridge as it traveled up to the cashier on another floor, the smells of each particular store—of the lunch counter offerings in Kresge's, the leather of the penny loafers—the sounds of a particular car as the driver cruised up Broadway, turning the heads of girls. The feel of our mother's gloved hands in ours as we entered the shops. Waves of nostalgia enfold us as we recall those days of our youth. It is a place that exists only in memory and old photos. It is a place and a time that will never come again.

When we see an old photo, it stirs memories that have been slumbering in the back of our minds. We begin to yearn for the past; we take out our memories, caress them like the precious keepsakes they are, hug them to our hearts and maybe even shed a tear for the past.

As I began to compile this book, I would listen as people gathered together and began to discuss the Council Bluffs they remembered from 1950s or '60s, the time before urban renewal swept it all away. Here are some of those snippets of memories people shared:

We had an actual city back then. It used to be such an amazing place. Now all that history has been torn down. I don't know why they ever thought that ugly mall was a good idea. Back in our day, the downtown was our mall. Oh, the good old days! That's the Council Bluffs I remember. A simpler time, and nothing was open on Sunday. Stores were open late on Monday nights. Downtown was always full of shoppers.

Do you remember how we would stop at King's for a Coke, then head off to Kresge for a dime's worth of candy and then wander through Pee Wee's? Kings had the very best cheese Frenchies. And, oh, the curly fries with a cherry 7-Up float! Their hot beef sandwich was just heaven. It was so cool to have the phone at your table and call in your order. Remember, they had the very best burgers! That was my favorite hangout, from King's to The Strand. That was my mall. It felt as if I lived half of my life on Broadway.

I loved going to the People's, or Beno's. Kresge had that photo booth—duck in with your friend and get a set of five photos. Laugh, make faces, never thinking it would all end one day. I found one of those photo booth shots the other day. We had such fun.

We would go to S.S. Kresge Co., to the lunch counter; they had the best chocolate sodas. It was my favorite store to go to. I recall going with my mom and grandma to Kresge's. I remember how it smelled. Every Friday, my mom would take me to Kresge's to pick out a new Little Golden Book.

And Beno's, gads how I loved that store. They had multiple floors and an elevator operator to take you where you wanted to go. Beno's was so old that we could feel the floors shake as we walked about. I remember the kid's floor at Beno's. They had a treasure chest, and you could pick out a toy from it. I remember they had those cool canisters the clerk would put your money in and send it up to a cashier—always fascinated me.

The soda jerks, buying a cold soda at the Sixth Street Market. There was only a two-cent deposit back then.

I always thought that Joe Smith's was a great store. A friend of mine got her wedding dress there. We got our gym uniforms, even girl scout uniforms there. They also had an elevator operator to take you up or down.

I always loved the "crazy days" sidewalk sale—always great stuff, and the sidewalks were packed with shoppers. My mother wore gloves everywhere, even to the grocery store.

The Iowa Store always had penny loafers and Converse shoes. The penny loafers cost $18.00 back then; it seemed like a lot of money. I guess it was, considering minimum wage was about $1.15 an hour. That would be two days of work to afford those shoes. But we had to look cool wearing them, especially in the halls of high school.

I remember going to movies at The Strand, the Liberty and the Broadway; it was twenty-five cents for a movie and fifty cents if you wanted to see two films. Popcorn cost only ten cents. There were double features on Saturday. Go to the noon show, and if you wanted to, you could stay and see them again. No one chased you out. I remember hearing about a young lady and her friend who got kicked out of The Strand for dropping popcorn over the balcony on people. Back then, they had ushers to patrol the aisles.

The Strand was so beautiful inside. At one time, there was a radio station in The Strand. We would go up there sometimes, and they had these huge 78 records that got left behind in the studio that was up there. When The Strand burned, it felt like that was the beginning of the end, allowing that vulture in to tear everything down, make he a packet [of money] *and left town before the paint dried on the new mall.*

When one of the theaters began to show less-than-family-oriented films, I remember a church group picketing the theater. Deep Throat *showing inside. I remember enjoying watching the protesters.*

As people pass away, so do the recollections of how the city was in their era, their youth, their time. The days, nights, parties, fun, entertainment—the joys and sorrows of living—are all woven into the fiber of the city with each generation as we live, love and pass.

The buildings of downtown could be razed and a new mall built, but the shadows, like spectral figures, rise insubstantial but quavering in the distance, like a mirage, as people remember the past, remember what once was with longing and an ache in the heart. Once gone, it can never be replaced.

One of the men working on the urban renewal of downtown made a comment as he looked at the old buildings clustered together along

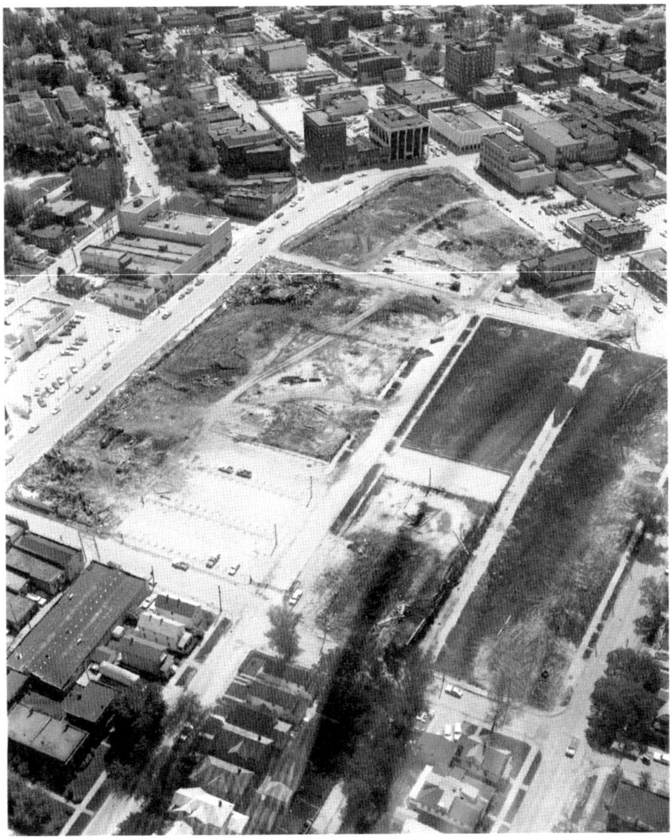

Once, Indian Creek meandered unfettered by the hands of the men who tried to tame it. In 1973, urban renewal promised revitalization.

Broadway: "There will come a time when Council Bluffs will regret tearing down of all these great old buildings." Another comment seemed to predict the future: "Malls are like people. They have a certain life span; then they die." At the time the downtown buildings were being cleared for the new mall, another petition came before the city to build yet another mall on the outskirts of town. With the building of the Mall of the Bluffs, death came to the mall that had taken the historic downtown.

The smell of the old stores, the creak of the hardwood floors worn by generations of shoppers strolling the aisles, the laughter of friends meeting, the pride of parents as their children grew and new clothes were purchased for the next school season, the fun of friends on summer afternoons—this is all the echo of memory now.

All we have are the photographs and memories.

BIBLIOGRAPHY

Babbitt, Charles H. *Early Days at Council Bluffs.* Washington, D.C.: Press of Byron S. Adams, 1916.

The City of Council Bluffs, Pottawattamie County, Iowa and the Trans-Mississippi and International Exposition Souvenir. N.p.: published by John C. Small, 1898.

Craig, J.P., R.A. Messervey and F.H. McMillen. *Council Bluffs Iowa.* Illustrated. Des Moines, IA: Miller & Watters, Letter Press and Binders, 1887.

Field, Homer H., and Honorable Joseph R. Reed. *History of Pottawattamie County, Iowa, from the Earliest Times to 1907.* Chicago: S.J. Clarke Publishing, 1907.

History of Pottawattamie County, Iowa. Chicago: O.L. Baskin & Co., Historical Publishers, Lakeside Building, 1883.

Miller, Lieutenant Robert L. *A Selected History of the Council Bluffs Police, 1853–2003.* N.p.: printed by Copycat Inc., 2003.

Palimpsest 42, no. 9 (September 1961).

Petersen, Calvin J. *The History of Fire in Council Bluffs.* N.p., n.d.

Prassel, Frank Richard. *The Western Peace Officer: A Legacy of Law and Order.* Norman: University of Oklahoma Press, 1972.

ABOUT THE AUTHOR

S.M. Senden was raised in Winnetka, a north shore suburb of Chicago. From an early age, history, reading and writing were passions, as was travel. Senden has studied, lived and worked in the United States, Europe, the Middle East and Africa, spending a number of years as an archaeological illustrator for various expeditions. She earned a master's degree and has studied creative writing, playwriting and screenwriting.

Senden has worked as a forensic artist with the police to identify murder victims in re-creating the face from skeletal remains.

Her publications include the murder mysteries *Clara's Wish*, *Lethal Boundaries*, *Murder at the Johnson House* and *A Death of Convenience and Other Short Stories*; two history books, *Red Oak* and *Montgomery County, Iowa*, published by Arcadia in the Images of America series; the short stories "The December Bride" in *Winter Wonders* and "Christopher's Egg" and "Hog Wild and Pig Crazy" in anthologies; articles and meditations in both the *Clergy Journal* and *The Word in Season*; a number of ghost stories published in various magazines; and bylines in numerous newspapers.

Senden currently resides in Council Bluffs and is working on another history, as well as a psychological thriller set in the 1890s.